Light in the

MY EXPERIENCES OF SPIRITUALISM.

BY

MRS. NEWTON CROSLAND,

AUTHOR OF "PARTNERS FOR LIFE," "MEMORABLE WOMEN,"
"HILDRED THE DAUGHTER," ETC.

LVX——LIGHT.

"The people that walked in darkness have seen a great light: they that
dwell in the land of the shadow of death, upon them hath the light shined."
—ISAIAH, ix. 2.

LONDON:

PUBLISHED FOR THE AUTHOR BY

G. ROUTLEDGE & CO. FARRINGDON STREET;

NEW YORK: 18, BEEKMAN STREET.

1857.

THE BIRTH OF HARMONY

PREFACE.

I AM not insensible to the probability that from a certain order of minds the present production will elicit a degree of ridicule and contempt. Nevertheless, I believe that there are critics and readers in abundance who are just and dispassionate enough to receive and to weigh evidence, even if that evidence tends to disturb their preconceived ideas and opinions; and of such readers and critics I ask pardon for the faults they will doubtless discover in the following pages. In so personal a narrative I fear some egotism is apparent,—and other blemishes, to which I should plead guilty, will hardly fail to betray themselves. Still I desire in this place to assert that my task has been fulfilled in the most conscientious spirit which it was in my power to maintain; that I have felt my way—so to speak—step by step, rigidly examining evidence whenever I have written of circumstances that have occurred out of the pale of my own personal knowledge, and in all instances undercolouring rather than exaggerating statements.

A third class of readers, neither a small nor unim-

portant one, will, I confidently hope, judge leniently of
the manner in which I have accomplished my under-
taking; I mean those readers who have themselves
personal knowledge and experience of Spiritual Phenomena. They will, I believe, rejoice to find any additions
to the band of truth-seeking believers who are willing to
give the world the benefit of their knowledge; and I
may assure such readers that though the friends who in
this book have rendered me the service of bearing their
testimony to the truth of spiritual phenomena appear
only under their spirit-names, choosing at present to
stand by my side as it were with their vizors down,
they are allies of such a quality that, with scarcely an
exception, their names, if uttered, would ring far and
wide with the tone of a rallying cry.

To all sorts of readers, however, it is due to give such
an explanation of some terms used in the following
pages, and to make such a brief assertion of my purpose,
as may facilitate their appreciation of those revelations
from the spiritual world, which may come upon them
with an air of strangeness and novelty. In the first
place, then, it must be distinctly borne in mind that
Spiritualists should not recognize in their vocabulary
such a word as "supernatural." They may term certain
astonishing spiritual phenomena "super-ordinary," if
they please, because the conditions under which these
phenomena take place are not those of ordinary every-

day life ; but to break a law of His own Divine Appointment is, we may be very sure, a thing the Great Lawmaker never does. Yet, though laws of the natural world are not broken or revoked, we see them every day superseded the one by the other, but always the lower by the higher ; and, under certain exceptional conditions, Spirit has the power of acting on matter, of making itself apparent to humanity, and of revealing, and from time to time revivifying, by the ALMIGHTY'S permission, those truths which it appears to have been part of His benignant plan never wholly to hide from His creatures.

I am well aware that the merely scientific mind will be likely to cavil at the use which is made in several of the spirit communications of the terms " magnetism " and " electricity ;" and in answer to such objectors I must observe, that we have been taught that these powers, conditions, or imponderable fluids, whichever they should be called, are to be considered as the conductors of those subtle forces—not the forces themselves —by means of which Spirit acts upon matter. This explanation is the more necessary, as, since the following pages went to press, I have become aware that terms familiar in our circle, and not to the initiated likely to convey any erroneous impression, have, in one or two instances, been used by me in a manner that may seem vague to the general reader.

I must also describe some circumstances connected

with the mystical drawing which appears on the title-page. Long before the First Part of this book was completed, I purposed that there should appear a Cross on its title-page,—a Cross entire, and beneath it that sacred symbol taken to pieces and forming by its broken members, separate and conjoined, the letters L V X— *Lux*, Light. With this object in view, I one day asked the young friend who is known in the following pages by her spirit-name, "Comfort," to draw a simple Cross with sufficient precision for me to place her production in the engraver's hands. She prepared immediately to comply with my request, only ourselves and a mutual friend, who is a seeing medium, being present. But hardly had "Comfort" taken the pencil in her hand, when she exclaimed, "They will not let me draw a plain Cross; see—see what they are going to do!" As she spoke, I could perceive that her hand had been seized by the spirit-power, and, with a rapidity far exceeding that of ordinary drawing, a winged Cross, springing from a heart, and with the various symbolic adjuncts that are found depicted, was produced. The second Cross, with ends ornamented with roses and lilies, was added last; but, before this appeared on the paper, the seeress who was present said, "I know what is going to be drawn; they are showing it me." Afterwards she described this symbolic Cross as having been presented to her in colours of liquid light, in something the same manner as the personal emblems mentioned in the following pages are shown : and she told me the roses were red, and the lilies the iris-blue. I should mention that I have myself seen a star of light follow the pencil's point of a writing medium.

In conclusion I may remark that, if in my narration of facts I have once or twice repeated circumstances already mentioned by my husband in the essay* he published about a year ago, I must ask pardon of those readers who may be acquainted with that little work : as, however, he and I have gone hand in hand in our experience of Spiritual Phenomena, it was not possible altogether to avoid intrenching on the same ground ; but I believe a single page would comprise all that on my part can appear a repetition of his words or thoughts.

C. C.

June 1st, 1857.

* " Apparitions ; a new Theory." By Newton Crosland. Effingham Wilson ; Bosworth and Harrison.

CONTENTS.

PART I.

PART II.

LIGHT IN THE VALLEY.

PART I.

LIGHT IN THE VALLEY.

—◇—

CHAPTER I.

INTRODUCTORY.

In writing of circumstances which have come within the scope of my own personal experience, I am not going to argue the question whether or not Spiritual Manifestations are permitted at the present day: I take it as an established Fact that they are, and a Fact not trembling into notice like some pale newly discovered star glimmering on the confines of visible space, but a Truth shining with a steady lustre, and, in many instances, like a vivifying sun upon the souls of intelligent, thoughtful, truth-seeking persons.

But though the subject in question is to be treated as an established fact, not as a disputed point to be argued for or against, it may be worth while to consider some of the circumstances which have disinclined one large section of the community from paying any attention to well-authenticated reports of spiritual manifestations, and to examine the influences which have prevailed over many persons who profess to have investigated the subject, but who, with a prejudice peculiar to the exceptional occasion, have resisted a mass of evidence which, if brought to bear on any mundane topic, must irresistibly have swept away all preconceived opposition and incredulity.

Few students of history, or careful examiners of the progress of Christianity, can have failed to trace the slow but steady growth of material doctrines as a strong antagonism to Gospel truth ; an antagonism, sometimes open and defiant, but more often subtle and specious, shooting from behind masked batteries of many sorts. In these latter generations it has become the invariable custom for " philosophers " to deride the " superstition " of their ancestors ; for biographers to ignore the traditionary credulity even of their pet heroes ; and for historians to reject the very keys with which they might have explained the puzzles of the Past. The result of this wide materializing of the human intellect has been such, that a spiritualist feels that, out of a hundred volumes which rest on our book-shelves, ninety-nine have been deprived of the most vital power which ought to have belonged to them, and if in the hundredth a few sparks of truth remain, they lie there unregarded, or are looked on as a blemish imbedded in the subject, like a dark vein in a sculptor's Carrara block.

But even a worse result than the materializing of our popular literature has taken place. The infant mind has been brought under the cruel bondage of this iron age, and the God-given instincts of a child's dawning reason, gleaming forth even through the corruption of our fallen nature, are, in the large majority of instances, ignorantly but systematically quenched. Observe how a young child of warm heart and lively imagination delights in the exercise of its faculty of wonder; or, to be more exact of speech, one might say, observe how a young child of this description delights in exercising the faculty we of denser souls call wonder! For, properly speaking, a child does not wonder at the marvellous and mysterious. Its young soul leaps forward with ready understanding at the first intimation of an unseen world, and holds the sublime idea of "God a Spirit" with a mental grasp so firm that sages might envy it. If, while this is still the case, children were taught

Religion, not from dry catechisms, but familiarly from GOD's Holy Book, wherein is full warrant for the belief that His Angels are ministering spirits for the heirs of salvation,* and, that their services being ordained and constituted by Himself, they are permitted to "succour and defend us on earth,"†—if children were so taught, were so helped to realize the truth of spiritual presences ever about them,—a truth their fresh hearts are so prompt to receive,—surely it is not foolishness to believe that there would be fewer fallings away from the pure faith of early years than we find to be the case; and fewer and less terrible conflicts with the sophistries of scepticism and materialism than now abound in the world.

But, instead of this spiritual teaching, so instinct with truth that the child's soul would, in most instances, respond to it as flame answers to flame, arrogant human reason sets about explaining the inexplicable. Not content with its own legitimate offices on which mental culture mainly depends, it dares to intermeddle with the affairs of the Soul, and, confusing and confounding First and second causes, generally conducts the young intellect into a bewildering maze, from which this same

* Hebrews, i. 14.   † Collect for St. Michael and All Angels.

human reason can never extricate it. No wonder; for human reason invariably searches earthward for its chart and its clue; and the Soul's guiding stars always shine from Heaven. A young child's best chance for spiritual elevation rests, humanly speaking, on its own wilful upward gaze, and determined rebellion to the tyranny of reason.

I would be the last to underrate the humanizing, civilizing influence of modern science; but, like every other material good, it has its limits, and it has its drawbacks. The great evil attending it has been the materializing the popular mind. It has been forcibly said by a great master-mind, that "a little philosophy inclineth a man's mind to Atheism, but depth in philosophy bringeth it about again to Religion;" and the diffusion of knowledge, as it is called at the present day, tends in a remarkable degree to the spread of a "little" philosophy over a multitude of minds; that little philosophy conducting them by the earth-spread chart to the bewildering maze of second causes, and making them therein so restless and so busy, that, by degrees, they forget the one great truth, that the motive power of all matter must be spirit. It is true that sentiments discarded from philosophy are permitted a habitation in the regions of poetry and art. For instance, it is thought a pretty conceit to say that "heaven lies about us in our infancy;" but only the Christian, who knows that his Master loves little children, and has declared that "their Angels do always behold the face of my Father which is in heaven,"* have any true understanding of the truth and beauty of that idea.

Surely it will be conceded, that the families in which a deep, and earnest, and spiritual faith in the great mystery of Man's fall and Redemption makes the rule of life—to be kept with such light and constancy as God's grace shall afford—form a small minority in the present day; and yet, perhaps, it would not be too much to say, that only in such families can youthful natures, in some measure, escape the materializing tendencies of the age. Many merely moral people, who are considered by the world respectable members of society, but are not imbued with any strong religious feelings, still have a sort of vague idea that religion is a good thing, and consequently desire their children to

* St. Matthew, xviii. 10.

be instructed in the tenets of the Church as by law established. But can we wonder that in the process of this cold teaching, all the vital force of Christianity is lost, and that young generations, so reared and nurtured, find no counterpoise of a living faith to the evil influences around them. No wonder the Bible is a hard book to those who refuse to receive it literally as well as spiritually,—to those who have heard so much of the peculiarities of " eastern phraseology," of " allegorical allusions," of " optical delusions," and are so in the habit of bringing everything down to the test of logic and the crucible of their own individual understanding, that they lose at last even the memory of childhood's faith, and its clear though infantile comprehension of the Omnipotent Spirit working by His legions of Angels. Many such persons would be distressed to have it said that they disbelieved Revealed Religion, and yet they do systematically shut out from recognition those very revelations of God to man which make hope most earnest, and faith most strong, and the glory of a blessed hereafter most absolutely apparent.

Surely there is a certain spurious humility that is wonderfully near of kin to ignorant arrogance, unlike as at the first glance they may seem. Though we are told that there is joy in heaven over one sinner that repenteth, people who do not deny the authority of that assertion yet often exclaim that "Man is too insignificant for it to be possibly realized that angels are keeping account of his doings." True, they do not deny that the Almighty Eye is able, from the heaven they place so far off, to scan our thoughts and deeds, but this acknowledgment is generally little more than an abstract idea, not an ever-present palpable reality. "I am too humble," says another, "to think that angels, or beatified spirits, could ever desire to manifest themselves to me; and though I know we are taught that, in former ages, angels did hold intercourse with men, depend upon it all that sort of thing was done away with at the time of the Christian dispensation;"—as if Christ's coming had put us farther away from God, instead of bringing us beyond all expression nearer!

Is it not more arrogant than humble thus to attempt to measure the Infinite Mind by the pigmy gauge of the human understanding, and to resist those instincts of the supernatural, those spiritual promptings, which are the heritage even of the rudest savages, but which cold, polished materialism takes upon itself to stifle.

Religion, as generally taught to the young child, is deprived of those vital forces round which the tendrils of the childish heart most fondly cling ; such tendrils fall back weak and torn, but seeking some support they probably now stretch forth in the direction of fairy-land. Religion a catechism, and prayer a form of words, do not satisfy the spiritual promptings of the imagination ; and, in many instances, for a long season fairy-land becomes a reality to the young intellect. Or perhaps I should write in the past tense on this subject. Thirty, even twenty, years ago it was much more strikingly the case than it is at present ; I confidently assert, that in those days children were frequently to be found on whom stories of fairies and genii had taken so strong a hold that the life of fairy-land was a much more real thing to their young hearts than the outer daily life around them. And it was so because, though not a true thing, it was in some sort a reflection, distorted though it might be, of those spiritual truths which were not yet trampled down in the young mind by the heavy hoof of " philosophy, falsely so called."

But, at the present day, it is considered so indispen-
sable to pour into the mind of the young student a
deluge of facts, that the course of fairy literature is
either altogether omitted, or is hurried through as if
the child must be denied even the poor frail rest of that
tottering fabric.   Later in the child's history, when
fays and fairies have ceased to charm, but while
Religion remains little more than a formula, the
Heathen Mythology, with its poetical personifications,
has often exercised a great influence over the mind;
witness how Art and Poetry teem with illustrations of
its Idealism.   But divorced from morals as corrupted
Paganism was, it is an ill scaffolding for even fancy
to build on ; and the study of its ramifications is often
the last effort of the mind before imagination droops
her wings, and becomes bond-servant and menial drudge
to the mere human reason.

Then come the press and the conflict of busy life,
the eager struggle for places and prizes, the firm grasp
of things present and tangible, the distorted view of
human happiness and human duties ; and just in proportion as material objects are unduly valued, and too
earnestly pursued, does the spiritual life of man wither

and corrupt. Of course, I am speaking of the great mass of mankind, the "many" who walk in the "broad way." The true Christian, who feels himself a wanderer on earth, and recognizes the world, under all its varied aspects, but as the scene of his passing pilgrimage, must be a Spiritualist in the purest and highest sense of the word. I do not presume to offer to such a fellow-creature one word of instruction, but I ask him to bear with me patiently while I state some facts, and offer some arguments, that may perhaps induce him to believe that the spiritual manifestations of the present day demand his especial attention. Fearfully as in many instances they have been turned to evil account by Man's Arch Enemy, it may yet prove that they are a boon from the Most High, calculated to be a grand agent in counteracting the effects of material philosophy, " compelling" wanderers in the highways and byways of cold Formalism, or rank Infidelity, to come in to the " supper-feast " of the Lord.

CHAPTER II.

THE "RAPS" NO NEW THING.　WESLEY—BAXTER—CARDAN.

MANY earnest persons who desire to exhibit a spirit
of fairness in argument, and are really anxious to
discover the truth, find one great stumbling-block on
the very threshold of their investigation, when they
begin to examine the phenomena we are discussing.
They say they cannot believe that messengers from
another world would adopt the contemptible method of
moving tables and rapping upon furniture as the means
of communicating with mortals.

Let us consider this subject from one or two different
points of view. Is it quite certain that spirits do not
act on us by methods more in accordance with our
notions of their dignity and sublimity? and if they
do, is it not common with us, instead of "entertaining"
the angel, to rebuke it?˙ We take down a book
at random, open it at some passage so singularly
apposite to our condition, that it arrests our attention,

turns the heart inward to tender, anger-melting memories, or awakens the soul to keen repentance—that cauteriser of sin,—or it stimulates us to some needful doing and daring—and we call it a "curious chance" that just at that moment we should have taken down that book, and opened it at that page. We do not so much as conjecture that it might be one of God's invisible servants that impelled our will or guided our hand. A mesh of apparently cross purposes compels us to defer a journey, and by doing so we are spared participation in some frightful catastrophe. We talk of a "lucky escape," or if sober-minded enough to thank God for His providential care, we do so with but a vague idea of His mysterious omnipresence, instead of the gushing gratitude and admiring awe we should feel did we fully realize the fulfilment of His own promise, that He would "give his Angels charge" over His people. Yet with once this clue of thought in our minds we might often even trace some links of the chain by which these unseen ministers have guarded and prevented us.

Again, a vision of the night, however strange and startling, is only fit subject for lightest jest or keenest ridicule; though we know that in ancient times God often taught his children by such means, and curiously enough generally made the dreamer one, the interpreter another. Imagination or a strange bed, indigestion or a hard pillow,—anything you please, is better reason for a dream than spiritual influences. Or if a veritable apparition shows itself, to warn, to teach, or to console, if it comes with as much of its heavenly glory as humanity can bear to behold, though awake, we vow we must be dreaming, and by our own mental disturbance become blind to the spiritual presence, because the agitation of our minds destroys that very condition which made us, for the moment, a spiritual medium. And when the tale is told, friends shake their heads and talk of "hallucinations" and "diseased brain;" and, probably, the next step is to drug the body into a state yet further removed from spiritual sensibility.

If, therefore, the masses of mankind are thus dull of sense to recognize spiritual influence as it is more commonly exercised, how are they to be gradually and effectually reached? If they call the result of tender guidance and support chance and co-incidence—if they persist in considering spiritual impulses as the natural emotions of their own hearts, or the spontaneous ideas of their own minds—or if an absolute apparition is set down as a delusion—how would the scoffers themselves desire a spirit to make its appearance? A very little experience of spiritual phenomena might convince such persons of the tender pity to our mortal weakness which dictates the familiar approach they so profanely scorn ; and deeper reflection than that which accompanies a first impression might even modify their views in regard to the dignity of the means lately so frequently adopted for spiritual communications.

Thoughtless is often but another name for foolish ; and perhaps there has been a good deal of thoughtless ridicule heaped upon the word Table. How apt we all are to undervalue common things! Is there no reverence for that mysterious table which was made by God's own order, as part of the Tabernacle furniture ?* No tender interest in that modern thing which must somewhat resemble the board at which our Blessed Lord himself broke bread, and bade His followers do the same in remembrance of Him? The vein of thought which opens up on rightly contemplating this subject is

Exodus, xxv.

rich in imagery and association,—so rich that I should have been little likely to hit on it myself, but owe its wealth to a conversation with one of our greatest living Poets, who, in answer to the ridicule hurled at the table, pleaded its sacred character. Indeed, the table is the household altar. Around it how often is family worship performed,—or in solitude the heart's orisons offered up! At the table we read, and thus imbibe the spiritual influence of master-minds ; or we write, either to fling our own effluence on the world, or, in the confidence of epistolary intercourse, pour out the dear thoughts of love and friendship. Round the table family and friends gather,—be it for frugal refreshment, or generous hospitality. Why, the phrase " our circle " is an idiom of the language, and, instinctively, congenial natures gather together to form it. Mark if discord unhappily arises, how the chair is drawn back, the circle broken! Who shall say there is not something about the table to which spirit may appropriately cling?

Knowing, however, the objections which are commonly raised to table-rapping and table-tilting, one evening, when in communication with a very high Spirit, I inquired what answer I should make to the opponents of spiritualism who resisted proofs of its truth on the plea of the trivial method of the manifestations. I may mention that I was in my own house, with no professional medium present, and was sitting at a small table with only one dear companion, who, less than a year before, had been perfectly incredulous on the subject of spiritual manifestations, but who possesses too candid and truth-loving a nature to resist accumulated evidence. The answer spelt out was—

"If we came with more solemnity, we should awe you too much."

Surely there is a most suggestive truth in this reply. All evidence shows that poor humanity, when not sustained by great spiritual elevation, and when unaccustomed to spiritual phenomena, starts affrighted at the first intimation of ghostly communications; and this is the case because the Gospel idea of Ministering Spirits has been so much ignored that terror of evil is the first thought which takes possession of the mind at such a crisis. Brave men, who would not have swerved an inch from the path of duty to escape a shower of bullets, have been known to flee in trepidation from an immaterial form, or else to take up

c 2

material weapons to resist it, as if ignorant that in spiritual conflicts the only sword is the WORD OF GOD, and Prayer the only buckler.

I am also inclined to think that there is some peculiar change which takes place in the individual when he first becomes conscious of receiving spiritual communications. I do not like to use the word "shock," lest it should imply terror ; and the sensation, the conviction I mean, is a sublime spiritual elevation, not unaccompanied by awe, but quite removed from vulgar fear. The very persons who, unprepared, would faint appalled at the sight of an apparition, unless they were materialists enough to consider it a "delusion," are brought, if God chooses them for Mediums, to hear spirit sounds, and see spirit sights, and feel spirit forms about them, as a part of their daily lives,—as messengers sent to remind them of Heaven and duty, to prompt their prayers, and show the littleness of earth. But this condition of the Medium is generally of slow growth,—often, I should think, only arrived at in the course of years, seldom more rapidly than in the progressive development of months.

And now perhaps the question arises, "What is a

Medium ?" and again we must be indebted to a Spirit's answer for a suggestive explanation. The following words were spelt out in my own house with only confidential friends present :—

"A Medium is one to whom GOD has given spiritual power during life to lead others to Him."

Undoubtedly a Medium is an individual who from some peculiarity of mind or body, or rather, I am inclined to think, from some peculiar balance of the material and immaterial powers, has a rare facility for receiving and showing forth those spiritual influences from which none appear to be wholly debarred. Even the deadest, dullest materialists, or most impatient sceptics, while utterly denying the communication of departed spirits with man, have themselves experienced presentiments, vague forewarnings of danger, or curious coincidences, which prove them to be in some sort mediums, capable of being "impressed" by spiritual imfluences, although such persons appear not to be accessible to the higher order of spirits, or at least not to show forth visible manifestations of their presence, except by a Divine fiat, which works what we are accustomed to call a miracle.

St. Paul speaks of the "diversities of gifts;"* and the "gifts" of mediums, though still maintaining their one grand resemblance, have ever been very various. For this is no new thing of which we are writing, but a living truth, that, throughout all ages, has, from time to time, made itself known and acknowledged, and, though laughed at and scoffed at by the herd, has never wholly died out from the heart of man. There have always been spirit-seers, and dreamers of spirit dreams, and even the "raps," so ridiculed at the present day by so-called "strong-minded" people, are chronicled by many a careless hand. In the biography of John Wesley we find mention of the raps which, in his father's dwelling, disturbed the whole household, and were confidently attributed by that sagacious family to a spiritual presence.

Again, in an erudite and delightful article on the Life and Times of Richard Baxter, which appeared in the "Edinburgh Review" for October, 1839, the writer finds a great difficulty in reconciling the powers of mind which Baxter possessed with his credulity in regard to ghost stories and circumstances which fairly come

* 1st Epistle to the Corinthians, xii. 4.

under the denomination of spiritual manifestations. Speaking of some of Baxter's theological writings, the author says :—

" It would be difficult to select from the same class of writings any more eminently distinguished by the earnest love and fearless pursuit of truth, or to name an inquirer into these subjects who possessed and exercised to a greater extent the power of suspending his long-cherished opinions, and of closely interrogating every doubt by which they were obstructed."

Mark the very paragraph which follows this laudation of Baxter's powers and habits of mind, and observe how the nineteenth-century reviewer, imbued with the peculiar incredulity of his own age, never staggers in the march of his sentences from any doubt of his personal infallibility ; never pauses to pay any respect to the weight of evidence which convinced Hale, and More, and Boyle, and Baxter of the truth of preternatural agency.

" In his solicitude to sustain the conclusions he had so laboriously formed, Baxter unhappily invoked the aid of arguments which, however impressive in his own days, are answered in ours by a smile, if not by a sneer. The sneer, however, would be at once unmerited and unwise. When Hale was adjudging witches to death, and More preaching against their guilt, and Boyle investigating the sources of their power, it is not surprising that Baxter availed himself of the evidence afforded by witchcraft and apparitions in proof of the existence of a world of spirits, and, therefore, in support of the fundamental tenets of revealed religion. Marvellous, however, it is, in running over his historical discourse on that subject, to find him giving so unhesitating an assent to the long list of extravagances and nursery tales which he has there brought together, unsupported, as they almost all are, by any proofs that such facts occurred at all, or by any decorous pretext for referring them to preternatural agency. Simon Jones, a stout-hearted and able-bodied soldier, standing sentinel at Worcester, was driven away from his post by the appearance of something like a headless bear. A drunkard was warned against intemperance by the lifting up of his shoes by an invisible hand. * * * At the house of Mr. Beecham there was a tobacco-pipe which had the habit of 'moving itself from a shelf at one end of the room to a shelf at the other end of the room.' When Mr. Munn, the minister, went to witness the prodigy, the tobacco-pipe remained stationary; but a great Bible made a spontaneous leap into his lap, and opened itself at a passage on the hearing of which the evil spirit who had possessed the pipe was exorcised.' 'This Mr. Munn himself told me,' writes Baxter, 'when, in the sickness year, 1665, I lived in Stockerson Hall. I have no reason to suspect the veracity of a sober man, a constant preacher, and a good scholar.'"

Admirable Baxter! who really had the good sense to consider that the words of a truth-loving, sober, scholarly man were worthy of credence. And we, at the distance of nearly two centuries, might do well to believe these stories on Baxter's authority. Nor is there any great exercise of faith necessary to do so; for there is nothing in them that at all contradicts the experience of modern spiritualists. The shoes and the pipe were likely to be strongly imbued with the magnetism of the wearer and user, and, consequently, to present, if they were mediums, the precise condition under which disembodied spirits appear capable of acting on matter. And the Bible, supposing it to have been much read or handled, must likewise have been impregnated with human emanations.

The Edinburgh Reviewer affords after all but an average specimen of the manner in which ninety-nine out of every hundred writers have treated the best-authenticated records of supernatural agency. They prefer any theory of delusion,—extraordinary credulity, inconsistency of character, superstition of the age, any really irreconcilable absurdity, to the simple fact that an eyewitness has told you the truth, and that the astute, clear-headed, right-minded narrator is worthy of belief.

Going upward on the stream of Time, we may allude to Jerome Cardan, the eminent Italian physician of the sixteenth century, a biography of whom, most ably written, has lately been given to the world by Mr. Morley. But, alas! this interesting and instructive work is not without the drawback quite customary to modern literature. The learned and diligent author regards as refuse some of the most valuable records left to us by his hero's own pen; and where he admits passages illustrative of Cardan's " superstition," he does so apologetically, with wonder and regret that such weakness should belong to a man who otherwise was so acute in his observations and clear in his reasoning.

Let us cite literally a few of the author's admissions concerning Cardan's abilities.

" As a writer he was at once learned and amusing. His quick, natural wit made him a brisk narrator, even when he was most garrulous: there was pith in what he wrote, and his works always sparkled more or less with those well-considered and well-pointed sayings, in which learned and unlearned equally delight."*

Speaking of one of his last works, one on Civil Prudence, and which was published after his death, the biographer says :—

" In this work it is to be seen that, as a philosopher, Jerome's faculties remained to the last clear and lively. There is the old terseness in it, and more than the old wisdom. When Cardan, in his old age, wrote upon any abstract subject and forgot himself, there was no trace of the warping of his mind; he maintained perfectly the tone and spirit of a man of genius and a scholar."

And this great man, who, through a long course of sickness, and sorrow, and domestic affliction, kept his

* " Life of Jerome Cardan," by Henry Morley, vol. i. p. 287.

faculties thus clear, is not to be believed when he talks of seeing spirits, and of hearing mysterious noises! Indeed, there is something pathetic in the way in which the biographer pleads, and assures us that though his hero was the victim of such delusions, he was indeed a man of genius, learned, and quick-witted. And as if to ratify his own judgment, Mr. Morley quotes in his preface some remarks from Tiraboschi's "History of Italian Literature," in which, after summing up Cardan's "delusions," the writer says, "A man, in short, of whom, if we read only certain of his works, we may suppose that he was the greatest fool who ever lived,—who would suppose, I say, that such a man was at the same time one of the profoundest and most fertile geniuses that Italy has produced, and that he made rare and precious discoveries in mathematics and medicine? Nevertheless, such was Cardan, by the confession even of those who speak of him with the greatest contempt."

The old story!—any theory of "delusion" rather than believe the simple truth. Nevertheless, this biography of Jerome Cardan is full of suggestive interest to the spiritualist, although the clever author provokingly says, speaking of the supernatural, " I have not thought it worth while to collect together all the stories of this kind related by Cardan." We wish he would think it worth while—to make a separate volume of them !

CHAPTER III.

THEORETICAL SUGGESTIONS.

THE great gulf which lies between Spirit and Matter must ever prevent our finding a perfect type of the one in a symbol borrowed from the other. Nevertheless, the old but beautiful image of the butterfly bursting from its chrysalis swathing, and thus typifying the final emancipation of the soul, may serve as a standing point round which to gather some segments of a theory. Not that I am so presumptuous as to attempt, at the present stage of my experience, to enunciate laws or establish a theory on the subject of spiritual manifestations ; but certain revelations have been vouchsafed, and certain explanations have been made in reference to these phenomena, and as such revelations and explanations harmonize not only together, but with my own experience, and with the experience of Mediums far more spiritually endowed than myself, they fall into place in my own mind with a look of verity, as if they were indeed to be the foundations of a stately fabric. Other minds may regard them in the same light and take the same interest in them, and derive the same benefit from them that I have done.

First, then, the spirits have declared that magnetism and electricity, though not spirit, are the media by which spirit acts on matter, forming, as it were, a bridge across the great gulf. Surely there is nothing derogatory to spirit, or to the ALMIGHTY LORD of Spirits in this idea! God loves to work by instruments; and when His mandate is to slay, we observe how He sends the tempest, the earthquake, or the pestilence to do His bidding. Can we, even by the light of our poor human reason, that is so often proud and rebellious, imagine any power more suitable to His benignant Hand, than the invisible and imponderable agents I have named?

Perhaps no system has ever prevailed in the world for any length of time, and exercised an influence over the minds of men, that had not in it—however mingled with error—some salt of truth to save it from decay; and the idea of the soul's union with the body, held by some of the ancient philosophers, was—

not more accurate than that taught by revealed religion—but more instinct with an appealing truth
than that vague, undefined notion entertained at the
present day by three-fourths of professing Christians
The spark of life! What a feeble, enervating, mis-
chievous phrase it is,—how suggestive of something
to be easily extinguished, and difficult to be kept
alive! Yet I think it will be allowed that it is
rather as a mysterious "spark" than anything else
that the soul is regarded by that body of lazy reli-
gionists, who consider themselves safe because they
take the Bible for granted, believing in its truth
without feeling it, but who,—as they have never been
tossed into the deep ocean of doubt and of ques-
tioning, to buffet on its waves, seeking rest for the
soles of their feet and finding none,—must surely repose
on their "dry land" with different emotions from those
of the strong swimmer, mercifully led at last to the
Rock of Ages.

Now contrast with this flickering idea of a "spark,"
—that is feebly conjectured to dwell in the head, or the
heart, or in a bundle of nerves,—the Homeric notion of
the Soul as a presence contained within the body, which

it exactly resembles in shape, magnitude, and features. An image within its mould is the figure used by the ancients. But this symbol may, perhaps, suggest an error; for a mould is supposed to give shape to the image it contains, whereas there can be little doubt that the soul gives shape to the body; and hence arise, it may be, those peculiarities of expression which we recognize in the face and the limbs, in the voice or the gesture of different persons, and which physiognomists and others have attempted to define by absolute laws.

Recent revelations, however, though more in harmony with the ancient idea of the eidolon, or image, than with the feeble fancy of a "spark," differ from it in some remarkable particulars. It would appear that there is a soul, or spirit atmosphere, which permeates through the body in life, and it is on or by this atmosphere that disembodied spirits are permitted to communicate with mortals. There is some reason to believe that it is on this atmosphere that spirit has the power of reflecting itself, and thus becoming visible to seeing mediums. It is spirit that sees spirit,—spirit that answers to spirit, and it is not beyond the fair field of conjecture that it is through this atmosphere that we often unconsciously receive spiritual and intellectual impressions. I am intimately acquainted with a seeing medium,—a young lady to whom these atmospheres are often distinctly visible ; of course she is a spirit-seer also, and she has seen spirit-hands gather this atmosphere about a table when a circle have been sitting for manifestations, heaping it up into little cloud-like mounds, for the purpose of making thereby, or therewith, the concussions or raps. Few persons, I think, who have often heard the raps will confound them with any other sound, or admit that they are easily to be imitated ; for the noise seems to proceed from the very body of the wood, and frequently before any sound is heard the table appears to heave and pulsate like a breathing thing.

Perhaps the atmospheres of different persons vary as infinitely as do their characters ; but it would seem that there are some distinctive properties in the spirit atmospheres of such persons as GOD has endowed with the gift of mediumship. The spirits frequently use the word " development " as applied to persons whose mediumship is being improved, and, in answer to an inquiry on the subject, we received the following spirit answer :—

"We remove the material magnetism, and give you spiritual magnetism."

It has also been stated that these different atmospheres are of different colours, white being the highest, and the order of succession being red, blue, and yellow. Wholly unspiritual people are represented as having dark atmospheres, verging sometimes on the absolutely black, and towards this dark atmosphere, by some law of affinity, evil influences gather. But the holy teaching which has accompanied this revelation sets forth that PRAYER can rend the darkest atmosphere, and that by the rent so made Holy Angels and Beatified Spirits are able to reach the soul they could not otherwise influence.

Quite in harmony with this theory, I find the following remarks in a curious and interesting little book entitled "Phrenology, Psychology, and Pneumatology, by an Introviser," which was published two or three years ago :—

"The psychical fluid, which I have before mentioned as pervading the whole being, is emitted from the soul, and, radiating through the body, envelopes the figure in a coloured atmosphere, somewhat resembling steam, only not so palpable : through this atmosphere we affect each

other, both mentally and physically, and by its agency
are produced the wonderful effects called mesmerism, or
animal magnetism."

After speaking of two other atmospheres, namely,
the mental, as distinguished from the spiritual, and a
third for the use of the bodily organs, the Introviser
adds that, when death ensues,—

" The beautiful atmosphere emanating from the spirit,
which formerly shone dimly through, and arrayed the body
in a cloud of coloured light, now constitutes the spirit's
glorious robe.   This psychical fluid is clearly visible to
all Introvisers, and in various degrees to many others;
and thus is explained the power of spirit seeing, which
is a positive fact, and no illusion of the 'distempered
brain.'"

The difficulty which exists with a certain order of
minds in realizing facts far removed from the pale of
every-day experience, without an explanation of cause
and effect, is often a stumbling-block with those who
persist in studying the Bible by the light of human
reason alone.   I hope it is not profane to suggest, for
the benefit of such persons, that the recognition of this
spirit atmosphere might account for some of the phe-

nonema to which they have hitherto demurred. When Moses came down from Mount Sinai, and " the skin of his face shone while he talked" with Aaron, so that "he put a vail on his face" while he "spake unto the children of Israel," might it not have been in reality that the saintly soul of the Hebrew law-giver was so sublimated by his recent conference with the Most High, that his spirit atmosphere became visible to all gazers, instead of remaining in the normal state of being only recognizable by Introvisers or spirit-seers ?   Again, we read of the First Christian Martyr, St. Stephen, that, when " full of the Holy Ghost," he addressed the council, they, "looking steadfastly on him, saw his face as it had been the face of an angel."   Possibly the glorious shining of that countenance resembled the light on Moses's face ; nor was the occasion wholly dissimilar ; for Moses had just heard the voice of the Lord proclaiming laws for His people, and Stephen was about to behold—being yet in life—" the glory of God, and Jesus standing on the right hand of God."

Certain mediums do sometimes see a glistening glory about a human countenance, which, though doubtless of an intensity immeasurably inferior to that recorded in

Holy Writ, nevertheless serves to remind them of it. I myself, though a seeing medium of very limited and feeble power, once saw what I believed to be this glistening glory on the face of a fervent Christian,— one who is a seeing medium of longer standing and greater power than myself. It lasted—or probably my privilege of beholding it lasted—for the space of about half a minute, and, during this period, there passed between us a spiritual appearance, rainbow-hued, which answered to a description previously received of the spirit-robe of a departed infant.

I am prepared for the smile of derision which will curl the sceptic's lip at this assertion. I know all that is likely to be said,—I have heard it so often,—of delusion, optical and psychical,—of disordered brain, of heated imagination ; but if I were greatly terrified at the shafts of ridicule, I should probably not be writing this little book.

Perhaps, however, it is too much to expect that the world at large should accept and weigh evidence on spiritualism with the same calmness and fairness that it might be inclined to yield were the subject, though strange, mundane, and capable of being objectively discussed. The truth is, that talking of spiritualism to those whose spiritual faculty is thickly incrusted with materialism, is something like talking of flashing jewels to one who has never seen; but the blinded eyes have often been couched, and the light let in, and none should despair of a human mind, sooner or later, shaking off its encarnalizing scales. It must never be forgotten that science, potent as it is, is essentially "of the earth, earthy;" and though human reason may by it build up a ladder of Causes, the topmost round, when all is done, is not appreciably nearer to heaven than the first. There is still the immeasurable gulf between God and His second causes to be passed. Man can control and make servant of the magnet, but can he understand the nature of its secret power? He can reef and unreef the sails of a ship to suit the steady trade winds of the ocean, or by the aid of steam can plough the deep without sails at all; he can discern the signs of the sky, but can he cause one drop of rain to fall at his bidding, or control the laws which spread out the black pennon of smoke that rises from the throat of the steam-ship?

The Spirit Atmosphere is to be spiritually discerned,

and is not to be tested like oxygen or nitrogen. The sun has its gorgeous setting, the sky its imperial blue, the grass its refreshing green, and the flowers their myriad-tinted robes, although the poor blind can see them not ; in like manner,

> " Millions of spiritual creatures walk the earth
> Unseen, both when we wake and when we sleep."

And human beings are either the stone blind or the half blind in regard to them. Only in heaven can the most highly privileged hope to have the mists wholly withdrawn, and to see spirit really as it is. Even the dim consciousness of spiritual presences, which so many persons feel, and their recognition by unmistakeable manifestations, may be likened to the awakening and development of a new God-given sense in the privileged receiver.

CHAPTER IV.

BIBLE EVIDENCE.

MODERN spiritualists are accustomed to experience scorn and contempt from two very different classes of persons. From the rudely ignorant, in whom the spiritual element seems all but extinct, and who are quite unused to look round and examine a new idea; and from the so-called learned, who by reason that their studies have all lain in the direction necessary to acquire a knowledge of tangible things, and of demonstrable facts, have minds perhaps as materialized, and as thickly encrusted with prejudice, as those of the poor unlettered hinds. Faith, as "the substance of things hoped for, the evidence of things not seen," is to both these classes an unknown faculty.

But there is a third class,—a class entitled to deference and true respect,—who refuse to investigate Spiritualism on principle, but oppose it, as I believe, from a misunderstanding of what it really is, and an ignorance of its might as a weapon in the hands of those who desire above all things "to convert the heathen." But by heathens I mean, now, the heathens of civilization, the heathens who dwell among us in high places and in low,—they whose judgment is that "light has come into the world," but that they love the "darkness rather than the light." The third class to which I have alluded are those earnest Christians who, having made the Bible their mental pasture from early years, and having found therein light and life, cannot understand that there should be people to whom its great mysteries present doubts and difficulties. Such Christians, when opposing the doctrine of Spiritualism, love to quote our Lord's words in the parable of Lazarus and the Rich Man,* where He represents Abraham as saying, "If they hear not Moses and the prophets, neither will they be persuaded though one rose from the dead." But a careful consideration of this parable will suggest circumstances favourable rather than otherwise to the belief that the dead do sometimes reappear on earth.

Observe the words imputed to Abraham, when the

* St. Luke, xvi.

rich man requests that Lazarus may be sent to relieve his anguish.

" And besides all this, between us and you,"—that is, between the dwellers in heavenly mansions and the tormented in hell,—" there is a great gulf fixed : so that they which would pass to you cannot ; neither can they pass to us, that would come from thence."

But when Dives says, " I pray thee therefore, father, that thou wouldest send him to my father's house : for I have five brethren ; that he may testify unto them, lest they come into this place of torment," Abraham does not say that Lazarus *cannot* be sent ; he does not say that there is a great gulf between Heaven and Earth, only that " they have Moses and the prophets ; let them hear them."

The distinction is surely most significant ; for, un-happily, it is no extraordinary experience to find unbe-lievers of so obstinate a character that the most startling revelations fail to convince them of a spiritual existence round about them, or of their own spiritual immortality. It is fair to presume that the " five brethren " belonged to the order of persons who, at the present day, are wont to declare that they would not believe in a spiritual

appearance even if they were to see one ;—the order of
rationalists, as they love to call themselves, who would
rather believe themselves the victims of a delusion,
and labouring under brain disease, than yield up their
errors, and become as little children under God's teaching,—that teaching which they have from time to time
resisted and rebuked, those errors which were hatched
by human reason when it

" Fell from service to a throne,"

and which, nurtured and reared by pride and presump-
tion, have grown to gigantic proportions.

But the heart which has rebuked the Spirit's teaching, and the heart which the Spirit has never yet
aroused and awakened, are in a very different condition.
St. Paul himself had " Moses and the prophets," and
yet he had failed to see Christ's face shining through
their pages until he was shown It by a miraculous
vision.   But Paul obeyed the first summons, exclaiming, " Lord, what wilt thou have me to do ?" and
without pause or parley, shook from him, like dust
from his feet, the prejudices of his life.   Perhaps something analogous to the conversion of St. Paul has been
repeated more often than the world imagines.

Our blessed Lord propounded the parable of the rich man and Lazarus the beggar, and yet HE afterwards condescended to rise from the dead and appear again on earth to ratify His promises and establish His Truth. And when Thomas the incredulous *desired to be convinced*, JESUS had compassion on his weakness, and said,—

" Reach hither thy finger, and behold my hands ; and reach hither thy hand and thrust it into my side ; and be not faithless, but believing."

As we know,—

" Thomas answered and said unto him, My Lord and my God ! "

And mark how gentle the rebuke for his slowness to believe,—

" Jesus saith unto him, Thomas, because thou hast seen me, thou hast believed : blessed are they that have not seen, and yet have believed."*

Now it seems to me that these two histories should always be remembered together. Our risen and Incarnate Saviour,—Incarnate in Heaven, and yet in Spirit with His people "alway even unto the end of the

* St. John, xx.

world,"—is as pitiful to human weakness now as He was when that renewed and glorified Body appeared to his disciples, and when He suffered the pierced palms and wounded side to be handled by Thomas. Why, therefore, should we doubt His willingness to convince those who are ready to be convinced, who wish to be convinced, who put themselves in the way of being convinced, of eternal truth, even by occasionally permitting one to rise from the dead for that purpose !

Nor can it be too constantly remembered, that God loves to act with instruments, and that His instruments, —often the very last that haughty human reason would have chosen,—are nevertheless always exactly adapted to His object. At present we only perceive in a generalized manner the tendency of modern spiritual manifestations ; but I believe that, in due time, we shall witness wonderful changes in the world, which these phenomena have been intended to inaugurate. There may be many ebbs and flows of feeling and opinion and doubtless there will be much error to be combated, and much suffering to be endured, for Man's Arch Enemy still walks "to and fro" on the earth, and Spiritualism is too high a thing, its belief ᴀ power too dangerous to the Prince of this World, for his emissaries not to mar and meddle with it, wherever and whenever the weakness and faithlessness of man permit their approach.

But Almighty Power perpetually overrules evil, and out of its issues brings good ; and therefore, though it be granted that Evil Spirits have been permitted to manifest themselves, and, with the subtlety taught them by the Father of Lies, to deceive, and distress many seekers after truth, the fact itself may serve as witness and voucher for much that a hard and perverse generation has sought to deny.

Of all the recognized stratagems of Satan, I confess not one appears to me so subtle and refined as that disbelief in his own personality and existence which he has infused into the modern mind ; a disbelief which is, in reality, the very stronghold of intellectual infidelity, and which blinds the mental vision to the coherence of the Bible, and to all that is most sublime and heart-appealing in the Saviour's sojourn on earth, —a disbelief which degrades His incomprehensible agony, and the spirit conflict in which He vanquished our Enemy to an unintelligible myth, and which passes the cloud of its own hideous darkness before the most transparent Truths of the Gospel.

There is a text from Isaiah* which is quoted by Christian opponents of Spiritualism almost as frequently as the parable of Lazarus and the Rich Man ; I mean that in which there is the allusion to "wizards that peep and mutter." But let us take these two verses in their integrity, and see if they do not suggest that communications to mortals were permitted from good as well as from evil spirits.

" And when they shall say unto you, seek unto them that have familiar spirits, and unto wizards that peep and that mutter: should not a people seek unto their God ? for the living to the dead ?

" To the law and to the testimony : if they speak not according to this word, it is because there is no light in them."

Does not this appear like an instruction for trying the spirits, scarcely less definite than that afforded by the beloved disciple,† which, though generally applied to the spirits of human teachers, is cer- tainly applicable to our unseen ministers, for unto

* Ch. viii. 19, 20. † First Epistle General of St. John, iv.

Christ " Angels, and Authorities, and *Powers* are subject." *

If, as I earnestly believe, recent spiritual manifestations have led many persons, who had looked upon the Bible something in the light of a schoolbook—to be put away with grammars and dictionaries—to lift it down from its dusty neglect with an interest that soon gave place to reverence, surely these phenomena have fulfilled a purpose nothing else would have been likely so exactly to accomplish ; and I cannot think it profane, in such instances, to trace and recognize the wonderful workings of the Almighty Hand.   There are many of the enunciations of Holy Writ which earnest-hearted men and women, real seekers after Truth, try to believe,—and, knowing their own weakness and infirmity, pray to believe in the same spirit as that which dictated the recorded prayer, " Lord, help Thou mine unbelief."   Who shall say that the God who heareth prayer has not chosen to answer that prayer by infinite condescension and a pitying regard,—by showing such marvels here on earth, that the kindred but greater marvels of the Bible find easy credence,

* First Epistle General of St. Peter, iii. 22.

E

even through the common avenues of human reason and comparison. The Christian's God is no longer only the Jehovah of Mount Sinai, delivering stern laws amid the flashings of lightning and the roaring of thunder, but the pitying Saviour, with His human heart that knows every sorrow, and snare, and temptation,—the Good Shepherd, that is ever ready to lift up the stray lamb and lay it on His shoulder. Man is harder to his fellow-man in disputing with him, and disbelieving unusual means of conversion, than Christ ever was in His rebukes to sinners.

CHAPTER V.

BIBLE ILLUSTRATIONS OF SPIRITUAL MANIFESTATIONS.

IT would require much erudition and Biblical knowledge to trace. even imperfectly the analogies which exist between the supernatural events recorded in the Old Testament and the experiences of Spiritualists at the present day. I shall attempt little more than to offer some suggestions which may open up the desired train of thought in the reader's mind.

Angels appeared, both to Abraham and Lot, in the likeness of men, conversing, there is every reason to suppose, after the manner of men, and in one instance, at any rate, accepting food. If we believe this,—and no believer ever sifts and parcels out the Bible, receiving one portion and rejecting another,—if we believe this, why is it we refuse to credit the well-attested evidence that spirits do appear at the present day in a manner recognizable to seeing mediums, who identify the same spirits as appearing to them, speaking to them, and otherwise communicating with them on different and distinct occasions? I cannot but think there is a sort of lazy profanity in rejecting the mass of evidence on this subject, which is already before the public of England and America. Why should people suppose that God's arm is shortened, and that His ways are less wonderful than they were of old—or decline the consideration and investigation of Spiritualism as " not worth while," deciding that persons, otherwise of sound mind and sober senses, are the victims of delusion, because the spiritual experiences of such persons are more enlarged than their own?

It was an angel in the likeness of a man that wrestled with Jacob at Peniel, and it may be that spiritualism will throw more light upon that remarkable encounter than commentators have yet received. An angel appeared to Joshua in the likeness of a man, " with his sword drawn in his hand," and, in answer to Joshua's question, proclaimed his mission, saying, " As captain of the host of the Lord am I now come."

It was the angel of the Lord that " stood in a path of the vineyards" when Balaam's ass was permitted to recognize the heavenly visitant, when God " opened the mouth" of the dumb beast, so that it spake with human speech, and "opened the eyes" of Balaam himself to discern the spiritual presence.* We are told that Balaam's two servants "were with him," but there is no reason to imagine that they beheld the angel; on the contrary, the sense of the narrative contradicts such a supposition. Had they seen a figure "standing in the way, and his sword drawn in his hand," they would surely have pushed forward to assist their master; for there is no mention made of treachery or cowardice on their part on the occasion, and three to one are odds reassuring even to a coward. But the words of the angel almost amount to an assertion that he was not seen of the servants, inasmuch as he makes no reference to them, but says,—

"And the ass saw me, and turned from me these three times: unless she had turned from me, surely now also I had slain thee, and saved her alive."

The phrase, "opened his eyes," or "opened his mouth," is frequently used in the Scriptures in a semi-typical sense, as expressive of a new power acquired. Then, as now, spiritual presences were spiritually dis-

* Numbers. xxii.

cerned ; and why should we cavil at the idea that at the present day God endows some of His children with the privilege of beholding spirits, while He denies it to others, just as in that olden time Balaam was permitted to recognize the angelic messenger, who was wholly invisible to the prophet's attendants ? Many people who believe this recorded history, because it is contained in the Volume which they consider sacred, often speak on the subject of spiritualism really as if God had lost some of His attributes of power and sovereignty since there took place those events which make up Bible History : " Yes," they exclaim, "miraculous appearances were permitted 'then,' but they never occur 'now.'" Now by what right do such persons take upon themselves to assert, and by what arguments would they endeavour to prove, this negative proposition ? It would be well if they would remember that there have been scoffers in all ages, and would question themselves narrowly, whether, had they lived in the days of the prophets, they would not have been the "stiff-necked" and hard of heart, failing to find truth in any Word of God that had not on it the hoar signet of antiquity It would be well for them to remember that one little Volume, which we can clasp between a thumb and finger, spans, like the arches of a bridge, a stream of time that is to be measured by thousands of years. The Bible is the record of God's dealings with Man ; it passes over in a few sentences all irrelevant matter, but enlarges and expands at wide intervals at those periods when God drew especially near to His creatures, either in deserved wrath or divine pity ; and angelic messengers and prophets or *seers**—for the words once meant the same thing—communicating with selected human beings were commonly His chosen instruments by whom new dispensations, and enlarged teaching of those dispensations already established, were announced and ushered in.

The history of Saul stands out with singular consistency and distinctness by the light which a spirit-message throws upon it. These words were spelt out in my own house :—"Saul was a medium, but he offended God by consulting undeveloped spirits."

It is to be observed that Saul consulted the Witch of Endor because, when he "inquired of the Lord,

* See 1st Samuel, ix. 9.

the Lord answered him not, neither by dreams, nor by Urim, nor by prophets."* And we can trace throughout his history, from the time that he was anointed King of Israel by Samuel until faith finally gave way to despair, simultaneously with the deterioration of his character, the gradual withdrawal of that spiritual privilege which belonged to the prophets of God, namely, direct communication from on high.

The passage† where the prophet Elisha prays that the eyes of his servant may be opened, so that he may perceive the spiritual army which is near, is full of spiritual teaching, and makes the believer feel with grateful gladness that, whenever our hearts and minds are truly in the service of GOD, we need not falter and cannot fail; for, though to our sealed eyes the angelic hosts around are still invisible, yet, verily and indeed, "they that be with us are more than they that be" against us.

But perhaps no portion of the Old Testament contains, within the same compass, so much spiritual revelation as the book of the Prophet Daniel. Daniel, who was apparently miraculously fed, miraculously pre-

---

* 1st Samuel, xxviii. 6.   † 2nd Kings, vi. 15, 16, 17.

served, and miraculously endowed with "understanding in all visions and dreams," must ever be looked on as one of the children of men most especially favoured by God. Few, even among " the goodly fellowship of the prophets," seem to have lived so habitually near to the spiritual world, and to have enjoyed such full and frequent intercourse with it. Indeed, his soul seemed to have worn its fleshy robe but as a loose garment, which scarcely impeded the spirit's flight, instead of the prison-like heavy covering that ordinary mortals find it.

And now observe—Daniel was especially a Man of Prayer ; and Prayer, either implied or expressly declared by the narrative, was always the precursor of miracles, prophecy, and dream-interpretations. Is it possible for the spiritualist who has been told that prayer rends the dark atmosphere which clings about the natural man, and that through the rent so made God sends ministering spirits to our succour,—is it possible for one who has been thus instructed to help tracing in the life of Daniel, and in many other Bible histories, the full confirmation of such a theory?

When Nebuchadnezzar, forgetting his dream, threat-

ens, with a senseless rage characteristic of the ignorant
pride of an Eastern despot, the punishment of death on
the " wise men and astrologers," because they cannot
recall the dream that is gone from the monarch's own
mind, Daniel is not excepted from the decree ; but the
prophet of God remains fearless and undismayed, only
we are told that he " went in and desired of the king
that he would give him time." This boon appears to
have been granted, and

" Then Daniel went to his house and made the thing
known to Hananiah, Mishael, and Azariah, his com-
panions :

" That they would desire mercies of the God of
heaven concerning this secret ; that Daniel and his
fellows should not perish with the rest of the wise
men of Babylon.

" Then was the secret revealed unto Daniel in a night
vision. Then Daniel blessed the God of heaven."

In these three verses there is a simple but complete
history of supplication, of granted prayer, and of thanksgiving ; but the thanksgiving is greatly prolonged, and
Daniel expressly says :

" I thank Thee and praise Thee, O Thou God of my

fathers, who hast given me wisdom and might, and hast made known unto me now what we desired of Thee."

In this episode there is clear evidence of spirit acting on spirit. The granted prayer does not consist in an outward objective event occurring, but in a thing being " made known" to the mind of Daniel. And this thing is that airy fabric which men are accustomed to think of as the very shadow of a shade,—another man's dream!

On this passage I will only remark—and I do it with a profound and reverential consciousness of the difference between one of God's prophets of old and ordinary mortals of the present day—that it has come within my own experience to have a dream, which I had never related to any one, interpreted by a Spirit tilting the table, as the alphabet was repeated, at the letters which made up consecutive words and sentences ; the interpretation being given without the dream—which had before appeared inexplicable—being described. Although however, the dream was not related or described by the spirit-manifestations, allusion by their means was made to its leading points, showing how these were types of qualities, in language so terse and simple, that

I felt the common wonder one often experiences when a riddle is solved—the wonder how that which has now become obvious for its truth and meaning could possibly have puzzled our understanding and defied our ingenuity to conjecture.

I have little or no doubt that the apparently foolish and aimless confusion of subjects so often remarked in dreams, is occasioned by the contest which is going on between good and evil spirits for the possession of our slumbering faculties.

The miraculous delivery of Shadrach, Meshach and Abednego, forms one of those striking histories that seize on the imagination in early childhood, and clinging tenaciously to the memory through life, shine out with more and more of awful wonder as we advance in knowledge, and learn to examine the details of their circumstances. Indeed, for a reason obvious to the Believer, it stands out pre-eminent among such histories; while the Christian spiritualist sees in it still clearer types, and fuller promises, and deeper meanings than are commonly mentioned in connection with it.

Long afterwards it was, and under another ruler, that

Daniel was confined in the lions' den, because he had persisted in praying to the one true God in defiance of the edict framed out of envy and hatred towards him ; but now the prophet expressly states the manner of his miraculous preservation, saying :—

"My God hath sent His angel, and hath shut the lions' mouths, that they have not hurt me."

Daniel, a dreamer and interpreter of dreams, a seer of spirits, was permitted to behold the angel who came at God's bidding to be His servant's defender and protector,—but why may we not believe that prayer is still answered after a similar manner? Wonderful escapes from imminent perils happen to some of God's people every hour that He holds the whirling earth together by the might of His word and His will.

In the tenth chapter of the book of the same Prophet, we find another and similar illustration of God's method of dealing with His chosen servants. Daniel has been privileged to behold a vision ; and to this privilege has succeeded a prostration which, however more intense, was probably of a similar character to the exhaustion which mediums of the present day often experience after striking spiritual manifestations have been vouchsafed, and which is to be accounted for by the withdrawal of the psychical fluid by means of which the spirits act. After describing the vision, the inspired writer says, "and there remained no strength in me;" and afterwards, in the tenth and two following verses, he continues :—

"And behold a hand touched me, which set me upon my knees and upon the palms of my hands.

"And he said unto me, O Daniel, a man greatly beloved, understand the words that I speak unto thee, and stand upright; for unto thee am I now sent. And when he had spoken this word unto me, I stood trembling.

"Then said he unto me, Fear not, Daniel: for from the first day that thou didst set thine heart to understand and to chasten thyself before thy God, thy words were heard, and I am come for thy words."

Surely, if we had only this passage for our warrant —and there are many such in the Bible,—it could not be thought unscriptural to believe that one of God's favourite methods of answering prayer is by sending angels and ministering spirits to our assistance.

"I am come for thy words," in the mouth of an angelic messenger, is a declaration of the fact.

In this same wonderful chapter there is further mention of Daniel's physical exhaustion, and immediately afterwards he observes : —

" Then there came again and touched me one like the appearance of a man, and he strengthened me."

Now this is quite in harmony with the teaching which in our own day has been received. Every experience we have had shows that, even in the performance of what we term miracles, God works by instruments, and keeps, not breaks, the laws His own Infinite Wisdom has framed ; and the being mesmerized, or, more properly speaking magnetized, by disembodied spirits, is one of the facts which have come within the last year under my own knowledge and experience.

" And behold a hand touched me," said Daniel. And on the awful occasion of Belshazzar's impious festival, when the golden vessels taken from God's own temple were degraded to services of idolatry, blasphemy, and debauchery, the prophet writes :

" In the same hour came forth fingers of a man's hand, and wrote over against the candlestick upon the plaister of the wall of the king's palace: and the king saw the part of the hand that wrote."

The whole of this impressive history is too familiar to need repetition here; for "Belshazzar's Feast" has long formed a favourite subject for painters and poets, and the phrase "the writing on the wall" has become the type of some sure prophecy near upon its fulfilment. Thus the story has become the property even of profane minds, instead of, like some exquisitely significant Scripture narratives, remaining little heeded except by Bible-readers.

But of the thousands—apart from that limited band, the really Christian public—who admire the picture and the poem, and talk learnedly of their rich colouring and fit Oriental accessories, I fear there are too few who, if put to the test, would avow a literal belief in the narrative on which poem and picture are founded. It may be they believe, in a vague undecided way, that there was some strange appearance on the palace wall that affrighted the conscience of the impious king, perhaps a miraculous appearance, but more probably some "coincidence," or some "natural phenomenon," to be accounted for by chemical science or perhaps it was the artifice of a professional juggler about the Court. But a spirit hand, that in the presence of that royal company was clothed with flesh, and so " came forth fingers of a man's hand!"—no, no ; in their inner hearts such sceptics do not believe this.

Yet surely such sceptics would believe the literal truth of the story, if they could really know that there are hundreds of persons now living who have been touched by spirit hands, have seen the writing of spirit fingers, have beheld the spirit hands become incarnate, and move, and handle visible objects, and have then watched their material covering—for such, in some sense, I believe it to be—fade away, even as a thick feather of steam apparently dissolves into nothingness.

I am one individual among these hundreds who have seen, and felt, and heard ; and I write this little book because I, among others, have a Truth to declare and proclaim, and I will not wrap in a napkin the Talent of Spiritual Experience which has been vouchsafed to me.

It is the more necessary for those who have been thus privileged to avow what they know, because life, at the best but short, is always uncertain, and it may not be part of the Almighty plan to continue these quite exceptional revelations, save at remote intervals. Be it remembered that the incarnated hands were dis-played, on the occasion to which I more particularly refer, to eleven persons at the same moment, all of whom testified to seeing precisely the same results accomplished ; but this is a different thing from ordi-nary spirit-seeing, and does not occur except by the instrumentality of such a powerful medium as Mr. D. D. Home. In his case it is evident that the spirits appropriate some sort of vital magnetic force from his body with which or by which to clothe the spirit members, and make them visible to every one present ; the fact that his *physique* permits this appropriation proves how exceptional that *physique* is, while the terrible exhaustion which invariably follows these dis-plays exemplifies, in a very distressing manner, the cost at which they are made.

I believe that many are sceptics with regard to revealed religion, mainly because, not having studied the Scriptures in the only temper—that of humble prayerful trust—in which the Spirit of God is likely to assist them, every step of their intellectual progress has led them farther away from the light. Satan has been well defined as the incarnation of "Intellect without God," and it is not too much to say that intellectual training without religious faith, and the lowly and sincere worship of God, encarnalizes the mind, and unspiritualizes the soul, as much as does a career of crime. But even such unhappy victims to "science falsely so called," and to the knowledge that "puffeth up," might be stayed in their headlong course, if the very logic they so vaunt, and the reason that they deify, could be made servants to the Truth hitherto denied. Such persons have always found it difficult to believe in miracles; but if they could once understand that what they have considered miracles are among God's present dealings with His creatures, and but the fulfilment, instead of the rupture, of some of His most subtle laws; surely it would then become "reasonable" to read the Bible with faith in the veracity of its authors, and "logical" to argue that what is now has been before, and will be again. It seems also both reasonable and logical to believe, that when one can in a manner vouch for so much of the evidence recorded in the Holy Scriptures, the rest should be received with confidence.

The New Testament is obviously even more full of spiritual teaching and suggestion than the Old, and there is one passage too remarkable in its resemblance to spiritual manifestations of the present day to be passed over in silence. In the 4th chapter of the Acts of the Apostles, verse 31, it is written : —

" And when they had prayed, the place was shaken where they were assembled together."

As proof that commentators have considered this circumstance as a miraculous sign from God, we find in the generality of Bibles, at the heading of the chapter, these words : " And God, by moving the place where they were assembled, testified that He heard their prayer."

If the Almighty condescended to show his presence and approval by the vibration of " the place " (probably an upper chamber) where the Apostles were assembled, why should we think a suspension of the law of gravitation, by the moving of household furniture, a too trivial method of proving a spiritual presence ?

CHAPTER VI.

BIBLE ILLUSTRATIONS (*continued*).

A RELIGIOUS writer of the present day, arguing in favour of spiritual appearances being permitted, cited to me three remarkable instances in which it is reasonable to suppose we should find some rebuke for, or correction of, this opinion, were it an erroneous one. The first is on the occasion of Jesus "walking on the sea," when the narrative is pursued in these words :—*

" And when the disciples saw him walking on the sea, they were troubled, saying, It is a spirit ; and they cried out for fear.

" But straightway Jesus spake unto them, saying, Be of good cheer : it is I ; be not afraid."

Observe, the disciples,—who, we must suppose, had already had opportunities of knowing more of the hidden things of God than any human beings had ever before been privileged to learn,—evidently believed in spiritual

* St. Matthew, xiv. 26, 27.

apparitions; and our Blessed Lord offers no chiding for their supposition that He was one.

After His resurrection a similar instance occurs, for when He suddenly stood in the midst of them, we are told,—*

" They were terrified and affrighted, and supposed that they had seen a spirit.

" And he said unto them, Why are ye troubled ? and why do thoughts arise in your hearts ?

" Behold my hands and my feet, that it is I myself: handle me, and see ; for a spirit hath not flesh and bones, as ye see me have."

And when Peter is miraculously released from prison,† the goodly company assembled at the house of Mary, to which he resorts, are at first incredulous as to the reality of his presence, exclaiming, " It is his angel."

The second of these three instances is by far the most striking, the most instructive, and the most suggestive ; for the risen Saviour, who towards the close of His divine mission would be little likely to leave an error on the minds of His followers, not only does not correct them for their belief in spiritual appearances,

* St. Luke, xxiv. 37, 38, 39.   † Acts, xii.

but sanctions it, by describing the difference between a body rescued from the power of death and a spirit.

This incident has an additional significance when we compare it with the scene* at the sepulchre between Jesus and Mary Magdalene, when our Lord says, "Touch me not, for I am not yet ascended to my Father."

Was that holy and incorruptible body, all newly risen, then in a transition state?

Perhaps no tenet of revealed religion has been so hard for human reason to receive, or has required so firm a faith entirely to realize, as the doctrine of the resurrection of the body. But believing, as we must, that the spiritual world is governed by laws as inviolable as those which rule the physical universe, the passages here cited raise up conjectures and suggestions which seem, as we entertain them, to root deeply in the heart that vital stem of Christian belief. It is in this respect that spiritual revelations have come, in these latter days, as a most merciful and benignant boon to comfort and strengthen the weak believer, and

* St. John, xx. 17.

to startle the infidel into faith. St. Paul tells us,* " There is a natural body, and there is a spiritual body ;" and that at the last trump the "corruptible must put on incorruption ;" the whole chapter in which these passages occur being too clear and distinct for there to be any doubt that the Apostle announced that the final change in the condition of the redeemed was to take place by the resurrection of the body. Some Christians believe that the soul remains after death in a condition of rest and oblivion until the resurrection of the body ; but there is much Scripture authority to be brought to bear in support of that opposite view which the experience of Spiritualists compels them to take.

I cannot but consider that the evidence of apparitions of the departed having appeared to the living is too strong for it finally to be rejected, even by the multitude ; and when people talk of delusion in these matters,—delusion on the part of men and women otherwise sensible and self-possessed, — surely they evince, first, irreverence to God in believing either that He cannot permit souls to return and do His

* 1st Corinthians, xv. 44, 53.

bidding on earth, or that He works on His creatures by deceiving them through their highest aspirations; and, secondly, a most unchristian want of kindliness and charity to their fellow-men, in throwing back to them their earnest testimony, and proclaiming it but a proof of weak credulity or wicked imposture.

Again, I know that the evidence of at least two trustworthy witnesses has been scoffed at and rejected for a reason that, properly considered, ought to have given their testimony additional weight; it has been rejected because they, authors of eminence, were writers of fiction, and therefore supposed to be plenteously en- dowed with the gifts of imagination. True, most true; but whenever "imagination" produces a fine poem, a beautiful picture, or a well-constructed story, we may be very sure that such imagination,—far from being master of the mind,—is only a faithful servant to the reasoning powers. No flighty intellect, liable to delu- sions and accustomed to caprices, can build up a work of art such as the world consents to honour; whereas the imagination of true genius is, however fiery, like a steed obedient to the curb, and that knows the hand of his master,—a fairy-like steed, that journeys hither and thither in search of the artist's materials, and is rewarded only by finding them moulded into an enduring shape. It is a silly fanaticism to rail against imaginative people : analyze the powers of an acute reasoner, and you will ever find he owes half his force to the help and illustrations afforded by his imagination.

I do not mean to say that I have seen the very faces of the departed restored to my view, but I believe certain trustworthy witnesses who assert that they have done so ; and I have myself been privileged to behold, —when wide awake, and in broad daylight,—on numerous occasions, certain spiritual appearances, which recall to mind some of the Bible descriptions of such things in a very awe-inspiring manner. But I must add, that I have been present on occasions of spiritual manifestations when spirits, professing to be the spirits of those I had known in life, have spelt out their names, and many curious circumstances connected with their histories which were unknown to the other persons present. On one occasion, information concerning a missing document was given, which on inquiry was found to be correct ; and I may mention, that it was information which no living person had previously been able to afford, and it was information which smoothed down family difficulties and disagreements. This could hardly have been the communication of an evil spirit, and it seems as little likely that a good spirit would have come implying a falsehood. Again, I cannot imagine that the messages we have received, messages urging on us the necessity of prayer, and faith, and holy living, could have come from Satan, or his must indeed be that falling house which is divided against itself. Still, it must be added, that we, like many others, have sometimes been deceived by false and frivolous messages, and have had reason to believe that a message commenced by a spirit ministering for our good has been caught up and finished by an emissary of evil.

PART II.

NEW EXPERIENCES.

CHAPTER I.

THE MYSTERY OF HAIR.—THE VISION OF THE ARCHES.

A YEAR ago I considered the foregoing chapters nearly ready for the press, and only by some of those links of circumstances which we are accustomed to call accidents was their publication delayed. Imperfectly as I felt the task to have been executed, I knew that I had earnestly endeavoured to fulfil a duty by writing of facts with which I was acquainted ; and, with a conscience on this point to some extent at rest, I prepared myself for literary labour of another sort. It was the period of a lull in my spiritual experiences, and I did not foresee that revelations more astonishing, more holy, and more soul-convincing than those I have yet narrated were about to come before me. Yet I still allow the first narrative to stand, feeling assured that, by thus doing, I am truer to my readers, and truer to myself, than were I to fuse old and new experiences together, and pour them out in a fresh mould.

Moreover, I am impelled to this plan by finding that my new and enlarged experiences do not prompt me to erase or alter any assertion or opinion I have already made or expressed ; on the contrary, I find in them a confirmation, with development and expansion, of the theory I have suggested and the arguments I have advanced. I find in them not only the most absolute proofs that we are surrounded by spiritual presences, which under ordinary circumstances are invisible to the mortal eye, but the most presumptive evidence that it has been from the creation of the world God's plan to work upon man's soul through such instrumentalities. Even our language retains the word "inspired" which ought to be a dead letter to the faithless thousands who use it. I find in my later experiences convincing proofs that these spiritual presences are in many instances the spirits of departed friends or relatives, and I believe that any intelligent dispassionate exami- ner willing to receive and weigh evidence—the more logical-minded he be the better—could not fail to arrive at a similar conclusion. I find in them full confirmation of that grand and beautiful truth that God, the Fountain of all law and order, never reverses or revokes the rules of His government; but that what we call miracles are and have ever been only the superseding of a lower law by a higher. It is because materialists are insensible to the vastness and beauty of this idea that they have refused to believe even the miracles of Our Lord, finding it easier to ignore the pyramid of human evidence which through the long centuries has held the record of them aloft for Christendom to acknowledge, than to believe that the course of nature was ever reversed. And yet was it more reversed than is the law of gravitation when a child lifts a stone from the ground, thus overcoming by his infantile volition and muscles the lower inert force? I believe not: the difference being but in the immeasurable degrees between the simple, the obvious, the well-understood phenomena of every-day life, and those subtle forces which the Almighty seems to wield behind a veil of mystery, a corner of which is perhaps in the present day about to be lifted.

When a magnet by the power of its attraction raises a needle, one law overcomes another; and the same thing occurs when a steam locomotive engine draws after it at more than race-horse speed a long train of crowded carriages. In like manner the laws of the spiritual world do—under certain conditions, and finding, there is reason to suppose, their *tertium quid* in magnetism or electricity—very often control and supersede the common laws of matter. And thus it comes to pass that I, with hundreds of others, am able to testify that heavy articles are frequently suspended in the air by invisible means ; that a musical instrument has been played by invisible fingers ; that, by those peculiar concussions which spiritualists agree to call raps, messages proceeding from disembodied intelligences are frequently delivered; and, in short, to certify to more interesting phenomena than it would be easy to catalogue or classify.

I have at this moment by my side records of communications from the spiritual world which, if fairly transcribed, would occupy a thick volume ; and sagacious readers, persons accustomed to examine new ideas without mental flinching, will, I am persuaded, acknowledge that the few passages which alone I shall extract are suggestive of great ideas, which, while simplifying and harmonizing with the divine truths of revelation, bridge over in many instances, even with the masonry of human reason, those great miracle gulfs before which intellectual infidelity stands at the world's end of its faith.

Ask a rationalist what he thinks of the history of Samson, and he will probably talk, as he imagines learnedly, of the "mythologies of nations," and suggest that such a personage never existed; avowing his belief that Samson and Hercules were alike fabulous creations, "representative types of qualities," and that the feats attributed to them were physical impossibilities. I would ask such a doubter to examine dispassionately the following vision concerning the mystery of hair, and then to acknowledge whether it does or does not bear upon its front the impress of a revelation of certain laws, the elucidation of which science has never yet reached.

I must observe that the dictation was taken down from the lips of the seeress in my presence, the gentleman—a clergyman of the Church of England—who was the amanuensis, being the only person besides ourselves present; and I allow the vision to stand in its entirety notwithstanding some personal details—omitting only names—because those details help to make more clear the description of Samson which follows them. The spirit who showed this vision is known to us by the name Vastness; but it is necessary to understand that these spirit names are used, not as appellations which are absolutely borne in the spirit world, but as a convenient method of individualizing different spirits, and representing to us their qualities. The sentences between single inverted commas are those delivered in letters of light by the spirit —the remaining passages consist of the words used by the seeress to describe what she beheld.

THE MYSTERY OF HAIR.

" ' I should not have been able to communicate with you through the writing, as I did once or twice, if it had not been that you possess the medium's hair, which attracts the spirit atmosphere towards it. Hair is one of the most powerful attractions which mediums have. Spirits feel attracted to them, because their hair drinks some of the spirit atmosphere. No spirit can come in contact with them without their imbibing through the hair some of the spirit atmosphere. Essence would be a better word than atmosphere. There is a mystery in the hair and the beard which I shall try to explain in time.'

" Now he is showing me a vision of the mystery of hair by means of his wife. She appears as she was on earth. She is not beautiful, that is to say her features are not regular, but she has a beautiful expression. She is standing, and as she stands her hair reaches nearly to her knees. She seems to have let it down purposely to show its length. It has a very beautiful atmosphere, and through that atmosphere I can see three guardian angels who act through the radiations of the hair. They belong to her. Superadded to them are many more spirits—I can count forty-five. He now says, 'That is the reason why woman has more influence than man. It is a more subtle influence than that of man, for man's is a more material power. For this reason a woman has power on her head because of the angels.* With the outer atmospheric influence you are already acquainted; the inner you have seen in the tableau of my wife; the innermost you will ultimately see, but not at present, for it is more subtle than your imagination could conceive.' Now he is showing the hair of —— and ——. His is the medium's hair, and therefore its atmosphere radiates very far. ——'s hair radiates still farther, and its influence is very

* 1st Corinthians, xi. 10.

impalpable. That of —— is weaker than either, but will become stronger.* He says: 'The atmosphere which you see being only the inner, you will see that it is in a great measure dependent on the health of the hair, and its fast or slow growing propensity. Dark and red hairs attract analogous spirits. The souls of individuals are analogous, and so attract spirits in accordance with their interior condition. Black and red alike contain iron in great abundance, and the outer is always stronger in people of that nature.' . . . . 'I was about to mention Samson and Absalom.' He is now showing a vision of Samson as he appeared when on earth. He appears as a young man not much taller than ——, perhaps five feet ten inches, although he hardly looks so tall because he is so beautifully proportioned. His limbs look rather rounded than powerful ; he stands in a very peculiar sloping attitude, as if he could not stand upright Now he has changed his attitude, but it is still sloping. His hair is rather light in colour, and falls below his shoulders. His nose is aquiline, but not at all Jewish ; neither are his lips, which are well

* I certify that this hair *has* become thicker and longer.—C. C.

cut. His forehead is peculiarly square, his eyes are very light brown, his complexion is fair, but appears sunburnt. There he stands. Now Vastness is showing radiations of light from Samson's hair, which attract hundreds of spirits who are ranged round him, and successively above each other until they almost resemble a column. All the spirits are remarkable for their hair. The hair atmosphere of each enters the other, and three spirits, who stand close by him and touch him with their hands, conduct the whole essence from them into Samson for any given object. Now Absalom is shown. He is very handsome and princely-looking. Vastness says, ' It was through this attractive power. But at last he used it for evil. He felt his power and became ambitious, and therefore the gift that might have been a salvation both on earth and in heaven, became the instrument of destruction to him. Even in this material world, it cannot but be acknowledged that women have great influence and controlling power, which may always be accounted for by their spiritual attraction and sustenance.' ''

A novice in spiritualism will very naturally inquire the manner in which the foregoing vision was presented to the seeress. I answer, through an oval crystal about the size and shape of a hen's egg. Accustomed though the world is to laugh at crystal-seeing, as an old superstition revived for purposes of modern jugglery, the world has before it the task, sooner or later to be accomplished, of restraining its laugh, and accepting crystal-seeing as a fact. True, the faculty is limited to a certain class of mediums, and the fact of these favoured individuals being in all ages a small minority seems to have served as a reason that by the large mass of mankind their existence has been altogether denied. But have not all great gifts, whether of genius or of power, been sparingly bestowed? Great poets, great artists, great rulers, have not been so numerous in the world's history that they crowd on our memory, nor have they ever jostled each other for want of space ; and it is really hardly more logical to disbelieve the power which crystals exercise over some persons, because we happen to be unaffected by their presence, than it would be, while gazing on a lovely statue, to deny that it ever could have been hewn from an unsightly block of marble, because, given the block of marble, we should have been utterly incapable of extricating a form of beauty therefrom.

The same spirit who showed the vision of the mystery of hair confirms, in reference to crystals, the theory I have already attempted to propound, namely, that the spiritual world is governed by laws as precise as those which govern the physical creation. Indeed, a little reflection in any candid mind must bring coherence to this idea, for it would be absurd to imagine that the Great Law-Maker is ever the law-breaker.

Speaking of crystals, Vastness says, " There is an influence in pure crystallizations that works upon the nervous system of some persons, thereby placing them *en rapport* with the spiritual world." And on another occasion it was announced to us that the crystal exercises a power with regard to spiritual vision somewhat analogous to that of the prism in its separation of the rays of light. Crystal-seers—and I know several —declare that it is a mistake to talk of seeing *in* the crystal. They describe that when a vision is about to be presented the crystal appears to expand, and then that it disappears ; nay, that surrounding objects seem likewise to give way, and only the spiritual world to be visible. My own impression, both from observation and report, is, that as the spiritual eye is opened the

material eye is closed, and that just in proportion to
the power and privileges of the medium is the perfect
or the partial opening of the one and the closing of the
other. Thus a weak seer does not altogether lose sight
of the mundane objects about him ; but under these
circumstances both sights are dimmed and very imperfect. It has been told us that all natural seers—that
is, those who see spiritual objects without the aid of
crystallizations—could by a little perseverance see with
a crystal ; but that many persons can see with a crystal
who are not otherwise endowed with spiritual sight.
Yet, though this is the case, one can believe that the
gifts are not so much separate as that the one is the
expansion of the other : just as in physical seeing the
long-sighted, clear-sighted man does not need the aid
of spectacles, which, on the contrary, are an every-day
necessity to the purblind.

Carrying out the idea of the proportionate closing
and opening of the physical and the spiritual sight, it
is worth remarking that in many well-authenticated
"ghost stories" in which the *revenant* has appeared
on the scene of its earthly labours, and seemed still
associated with mundane affairs, the incident has been

infinitely less elevating or impressive than are those sublimer revelations in which the seer has been lifted above the accessories of the world, and taught by a purely spiritual vision. The weakness, the inferiority, there is every reason to suppose, consists in the infirmity of the medium, whose seeing faculty is not developed to higher experiences. History and biography are replete with cases in point.

Yet it must be borne in mind that as spirit appears to see, hear, feel, to *know*, in fact, without the aid of the bodily organs, its knowledge will always include a comprehension of any mundane accessories needful to the perfection of a vision, even if they be accessories capable of being perceived by the physical eye. Hence there will perhaps always be some difficulty in deciding how far the bodily organ is used in spirit-seeing. The phenomena, however, of clairvoyance, and even of ordinary dreaming, suggest how completely the spirit eye can see, totally unaided by outer light, which is necessary to the use of the physical organ.*

* I am not ignorant that the researches and writings of Baron Reichenbach, Professor Gregory, and others, have brought before the public a mass of very curious facts in connection with the action of crystals on the human body. Yet, so far as I know, the inves-

Before dismissing the subject of crystal-seeing, I will extract the description of a vision witnessed in my presence by the seeress to whom I have already alluded,

tigations of scientific men have not led them much beyond the observation of the magnetic effects produced on certain patients by contact with crystals, and the satisfactory proofs they have obtained of the luminosity of crystals to "sensitive" persons. Nevertheless, these admissions are a good foundation on which to build a grander structure. Professor Gregory admits that there is already demon- strated "the existence of a force, influence, or imponderable fluid, whatever name be given to it, which is distinct from all the known forces, influences, imponderable fluids, such as heat, light, elec- tricity, magnetism, and from the attractions, such as gravitation or chemical attraction. But it is highly analogous to the other impon- derables, and, as we have seen, is found associated with them." It is found associated with them. Yes, because, in all probability, light, heat, magnetism, electricity, and those occult forces which reveal to us chemical affinities, belong to the highest and subtlest of all *material* powers ; whereas, what science has chosen to call the odyle force may be the grossest of the *spiritual* qualities. There is a point in the physical kingdoms where vegetable ends and animal begins, and it is reasonable to believe that the mighty chain of God's crea- tions is without a broken link. Spiritualists, however, will probably prefer accepting the revelation already given with regard to mag- netism and electricity (see page 31) to considering those wonderful forces as simply ordinary material properties.

I am also aware that some persons will acknowledge that certain effects may be produced by crystals, but will refer them all to the production of a natural state of clairvoyance. Let this be admitted, if they like ; but then it would be necessary to discuss what are the phenomena of clairvoyance, mesmerism, and even ordinary dream- ing ; and spiritualists must maintain that they all owe their individual characteristics to a directing spiritual agency.

it being written at the moment from her dictation. To those unfortunates who do not recognize the fulness and majesty of Symbolic Teaching it will perhaps seem dull and uninteresting ; but I rejoice to know that there are many minds far differently constituted,—minds learned in the schools and diligent enough in the beaten track of wordy discourse and clamorous argument, which yet have come round at last to a finer humility than that of a child, recognizing that the meanest of God's works contain inexhaustible arcana, and are instinct with lessons for the wisest to learn. Especially does the poet or the philosophic student of history know that the deepest thoughts and the most profound truths are those which language most commonly weakens or dilutes ; whereas an apt symbol of a truth is inde-structible—eternal—ever fresh and new to each new generation—and to the wise never trite, because a per-fect symbol contains within itself the elements of adap-tation and development. The earnest-hearted of all creeds, I believe, feel that the world is indeed "written over by the finger of God," and it may well prove an occupation for us in eternity to decipher that writing.

Before proceeding to what our circle has called

"The Vision of the Arches," it may be interesting to know that in the spiritual world colours are the representatives of qualities. Blue represents Wisdom, and is generally the first colour seen by spirit-seers; red signifies Love, which follows wisdom; and yellow typifies Light and Life. On a particular occasion Vastness gave us the following message :—" To man was given wisdom, the first spiritual gift, and that is represented in the spiritual world by the colour blue. Wisdom gives government, and therefore blue is always a governing type. The woman, the last created terrestrial being, approaches more nearly to the celestial than any form of the terrestrial creation. Therefore, the first spiritual gift given to the woman is love, for she is the representative of it. Love rules. So the union of love and wisdom gives dominion—the type of which is purple,—and unto humanity was given dominion over all created things and beings. But woman also represents the church. The church is militant, and woman is militant; when the church is triumphant, woman will be triumphant."

VISION OF THE ARCHES.

" I appear to see some place in the spirit world which all the spirits are showing me. There is an immense arch so high that I cannot describe the height. The arch is made of pure crystal, and is not plainly cut, but is profusely decorated, something like a florid Gothic arch. There is an obelisk in the centre which seems to be made of one sapphire, and which divides the arch into two roads, as it were. The obelisk is octagonal. Now I see a succession of arches and obelisks. I can count twenty: they make two avenues, and I appear to see with one eye down one avenue, and with the other eye down the other. They are not all alike. The first is sapphire, the next ruby, the next topaz, then there comes a kind of amethyst purple; the two next are more opaque, something like cornelian, white and red. They finish just as they began. Now the arches all open and disclose an immense domed room, something like a chapter-house, of an octagonal form—it is profusely decorated with jewels and gold. In the midst are three huge rubies, although they seem small in comparison with the building. They are as large as the round table. On them is supported an immense crystal slab. The spirits now heap on the slab, books, and jewels, and crystals, as if they poured them on it by armfuls : then they separate the books, the coloured jewels, and the crystals into three distinct heaps. Now there is a throng of spirits coming in, several hundreds, and they are all dressed differently. The floor looks like an iceberg with the sun shining on it. The walls are gorgeously coloured, and peculiarly decorated. First a blue colour runs round the room, beginning with dark blue, and fading almost to white. Above the blue there are thousands of ornaments like silver doves, each with a light in its mouth. Above them is a very faint shade of gold, and all round are discs of a deeper gold, and in the discs appear the likenesses of all the animals in creation. The lion, tiger, leopard, and all the cat tribe are in one disc—the dogs are in another, and so on to the butterflies. Above them is a similar series of discs filled with flowers, all grouped together in the same way. In the centre of the dome there is something very wonderful ; it revolves constantly and appears to uphold the whole building. It is not supported from below. There is first a white atmosphere, then round it is a grey sphere, and a black spike seems to run through it. The spirits say that it typifies the sustaining power of God in the universe. The books represent man's mind, the coloured jewels represent the material body, and the clear crystals the soul. The three rubies are the sustaining Love of God, and the crystal represents His Spirit covering that love. Now the spirits have come into the room and are going to show something. They point to the row of white doves, and say that they show the altitude to which the mind and reason of man can attain. But the animals and flowers are placed above them to signify that man has not comprehended them or their purposes. Why animals live or flowers bloom he knows not, except that it is the will of God that they should do so. This is one of the things that we wish to teach, and this is a kind of introductory chapter. There are eight sides to the room, and the corner and centre doves of each side are larger than the others. These are the poets and prophets. The spirits are now throwing strong ropes over some of the doves, two on each side, and fasten them to the ground. They say that the ropes represent the fetters that science weaves for itself, even beyond the power of the prophets and poets to elevate them. They are

trying to raise the ropes, but cannot. The central
moving sphere now is drawn down and touching the
ropes, and the spirits say that although matter cannot
ascend to heaven, heaven descends to matter. Now
the vision appears to be growing dim, as if a mist were
coming over it, filling up one arch after the other.
The white mist has filled almost all now, and our own
guardian angels are standing under the last arch.
Vastness says, ' The forty arches represent forty years
of man's outer life, in which man's spirit ought to
attain perfection, and if it does not do so in that
time it never will in this life. The beginning, like
the end, represents the twofold childhood, or recipient
state of a child.' Now all the arches are gone. I see
mountains and cataracts, caverns within the mountains, and abundance of rushing water. Syria and
other spirits have come in. Innocence says, ' It would
be better could all spirits live on earth enshrined in
the body for the space of forty years, because they
would take a different place in the spirit spheres.
To die young is not so great a boon. Length of days
is one of the greatest of earthly blessings, because it
gives the soul time to expand. God's blessing should

be appreciated, and you should strive in every way to lengthen your life, however useless it may appear in your eyes. Though you may have done much in twenty years, you may more than treble it in forty. The spirit is, like the world, written over by the finger of God, and the longer it remains enshrined in the flesh, the more permanent becomes the impress of the writing. He has traced His words in flaming light upon the skies, in living greenery upon the earth, and in changing shades of white and blue upon the sea.'"

CHAPTER II.

SPIRIT WRITING.—SYMBOLIC SPIRIT DRAWING.

WE all know how very differently the same statements or the most similiar experiences affect different
minds; and it cannot be expected that all natures
should follow out the premises, equally accepted, in
the same track and to the same far-extending conclusions. Nevertheless, it has been observed, not only by
myself, but by many of my spiritualist friends, that
while we cannot call to mind a single instance of a
candid and patient investigator of modern spiritual
phenomena remaining unconvinced of their reality,
the calm earnestness with which the investigation has
been pursued, and the ready candour with which
prejudices no longer tenable have been laid aside,
have always shown themselves just in proportion to
the logical capacities of the mind, and its power of
reasoning from and by analogies. I know there is a
very general opinion afloat, that the believers in

modern spiritual manifestations consist of silly, idle men and women, people in search of a new excitement, and ready to take up with any novelty that may provoke a sensation ; I beg leave to say, that, so far as the experience of the last three years permits me to judge, it is precisely this latter class of persons who shrink away affrighted from the subject, refusing to believe and declining to investigate. They want a pleasant, gentle, unfatiguing excitement, something that goes with the grain of their preconceived notions and feelings ; but demur altogether at having their souls deeply stirred, and the opinions of a life violently uprooted. They are willing to elaborate a little—though only a little—their old time-honoured ideas, but to build up the bright fabric of a new knowledge requires an effort of thought, involving mental throes, and such people seek pastime, not labour.

No! they who are foremost among the believers in modern spiritual manifestations are by no means of the class denominated idle or silly; and though, in some details which it will now be necessary to give, I shall shield the personalities of my friends under those "spirit names" which have been given them from the spirit world to mark their individualities, it is no breach of confidence to avow that with hardly an exception their human names as well as those of many other spiritualists would be recognized as famous in the world of art and letters; as eminent among clear-headed, high-minded, and indefatigable workers for humanity; or as those of brave defenders of their country whom their Sovereign delighteth to honour.

These are the orders of people who have been found candid and patient to investigate, and awed, and yet supremely grateful and happy, as the grand truth of the reality of spiritual phenomena has dawned upon their minds; and among these personages two peculiar spiritual gifts appear to be widely developing—namely, drawing and writing mediumships.

By a Drawing Medium I mean one whose hand is seized by the spirit power, and, a pencil being placed between the fingers, is made to execute a drawing more or less finished without the automatic artist exerting his own will, or knowing from minute to minute what is coming. I have seen such drawings in course of execution more times than I can remember. By a Writing Medium I indicate a person whose hand is similarly seized, but for the purpose of writing words and sentences, usually, in whatever language they may be, in a writing widely different from the ordinary handwriting of the medium, and, as in the case of the drawing, without any volition or mental dictation on the part of the operator.

There is, however, a second sort of writing, which, taken in connection with the sublime teaching that has been conveyed through it, affords one of the most striking and conclusive evidences of disembodied Intelligences communicating with embodied humanity that have yet been recorded. Three years ago a young lady, a medium whom I shall designate "The Rose," was taught by spirits, directly communicating with her, three spirit languages; that is to say, she was taught the meaning of certain characters and inflexions, which are quite distinct, so far as I have been able to ascertain, from any known languages ancient or modern. She sometimes wondered for what purpose this knowledge had been imparted; but her experience of spiritual things was already so amazing, and her religious faith in connection with them so strong, that she never disquieted herself on the subject, but waited patiently to see what use would be made of her strange acquirements. Introduced last autumn to another medium, a young lady whom we have been instructed to call "Comfort," "The Rose" discovered that her new acquaintance wrote by spirit power the first-taught of those mystic languages. For some months Comfort had been rapidly developing as a drawing and writing medium, her early performances having been comparatively crude, and sheets of paper having been destroyed under the impression that they were covered with mere scribbling. There is now little or no doubt that what appeared scribbling consisted of the first attempts at writing a spirit language; for it is remarkable that when the hand is first seized, either for the purpose of drawing or writing, the result is generally more or less rude and imperfect, as if the guiding spirit required use and practice with the human mechanism. After all, this fact is but analogous to our common experience. When either child or adult first learns a new manual labour—be it writing or some other art—the eye may be quick to perceive, and the will strong to indicate what should be executed, but until the guiding mind has acquired by practice the full use and command of the hand, neat execution will not follow the directing will. In like manner does the spirit who draws or writes through a medium appear to require practice with the chosen instrument, the difference, perhaps, only consisting in the fact that another spirit instead of our own directs our hand for the time being.

Subsequently five other mediums, all personally known to me, have developed as writers of the first spirit language; and one of them, an author of repute and M.A. of the University of Oxford, has also on two or three occasions written in the second of the spirit languages, the characters of which seem mainly composed of dots. Be it remembered that the writers of a spirit language do not understand its meaning; and wonderful wisdom is evinced in that plan which makes the writer one, the interpreter another. Those writing mediums whose hands are moved to write only in their mother tongue acknowledge that they are constantly perplexed, and find continually that the communications are impeded or broken off by the action of their own minds guessing what is coming, as word after word drops from the pen. Evidently this interference of the medium's own mind with the spirit action disturbs the subtle forces which are at work. But when the spirit language is produced the case is wholly different, for the medium cannot even conjecture the meaning of the hieroglyphics his hand traces, and consequently his mind remains in a passive state on the subject, no way interfering with the action of his pen.

Spiritualists may differ about the degree of pure and Divine inspiration which was the privilege of Emanuel Swedenborg ; but none are likely to deny that he was one of the most extraordinary mediums of whom the world has any record. Long after I was acquainted with spirit writing, I came upon a passage in Swedenborg's "Heaven and Hell," which seems to me so curious in connection with the subject that I now extract it.

" Writing in the inmost heaven consists of various inflected and circumflected forms, and the inflexions and circumflexions are according to the form of heaven. By these the angels express the arcana of their wisdom, many of which cannot be uttered by words ; and, what is wonderful, the angels are skilled in such writing without being taught, for it is implanted in them like their speech . . . . and therefore this writing is heavenly writing, which is not taught, but inherent, because all extension of the thoughts and affections of the angels, and thus all communication of their intelligence and wisdom, proceeds according to the form of heaven, and hence their writing also flows into that form. I have been told that the most ancient people on this earth wrote in the same manner before the invention of letters, and that it was transferred into the letters of the Hebrew language, which in ancient times were all inflected. Not one of them had the square form in use at this day; and hence it is that the very dots, iotas, and minutest parts of the Word contain heavenly arcana and things Divine."

This is not the place for a discussion on Swedenborg's writings and privileges, although whenever his name is mentioned it is well to remember that he himself never attempted to found or to be the head of a sect. On his death-bed he received the communion according to the rites of that branch of the Christian church to which through life he had belonged; and had not his followers narrowed the usefulness of his works by setting them forth as exclusive and peculiar, their mingled yarn of gold and frieze might long ago have been considered rather the property of a Church Universal, than the rallying point of a party.

I now proceed to give a translation from the spirit language, together with a *fac-simile* of the original. It will be observed that when the writer's hand was seized a few words of English were first written, and that the rough drawing of a wheel is introduced among the writing. The whole is somewhat reduced in size, the original having occupied half a sheet of ordinary note-paper. The writer, a gentleman, bears the spirit name " Expansion."

" The God-power in creation is represented by a wheel ever revolving and evolving. God is the Creator and Sustainer, the Mover and the Fixer, the Transmuter and the Elevator, because in His nature is contained the perfection of all essences, beings, and things that have been or are to be. All His works form circles and cycles. For the last seventy years the scientific segment of the wheel has been presented to this earth ; hence an accumulation, in the treasure-house of science, of dead and material facts, which are now at the present moment in a state analogous to that of the dry bones in the valley of Jehoshaphat in the vision of Ezekiel—an

SPIRIT WRITING

exceeding multitude, but very dead. Now the wheel of God's being is revolving so that the spiritualizing, which is the vivifying power, will pass over this same section of His outer creation, giving life, which is spirit, giving poetry, which is mind, to this inert and before immovable mass. Vivified and poetized, these facts of science will become popular: they will expand, and instead of being material, they will become the bodies of great mental and spiritual ideas. By the outer images thus accumulated by the outer mind, God will dower His mental and His spiritual poets and messengers. From these facts they will derive images of the true God-nature, which will no longer appertain to the outer, but will become the vehicles of interior or God-thoughts to the most outer of mind; for God is now showering His mental baptism upon science and the scientific mind. It will take about thirty years to perfect this mental baptism, and then the spiritual life and light will come in their fulness and their brightness. Science being the body, mentalized science the representative of the dual nature of God, after the lapse of thirty years His spirit will be potent to triunize the whole to Himself."

I do not think such a passage as the foregoing requires any comment from my pen; yet I would draw attention to the use which is made of the words outer and inner. Outer, Inner, and Innermost are terms which frequently occur in our spirit messages, and, distinguished broadly as indicating body, mind, and soul, they are often expressive of the most subtle and suggestive meanings.

The next specimen I present of combined spirit drawing and writing is wholly of a symbolic character. It was executed through the hand of a gentleman who has become a medium within the last four months, and who bears the spirit name of "Confidence." I should mention that Expansion and Confidence are unacquainted with each other, never to the present moment having met. I need not repeat that the hand was moved by a spirit, without any volition or knowledge of what was to be executed on the medium's part; for I would wish my readers to understand that this has always been the case with the *uncoloured* drawings and writings reproduced in this volume.

The following is an explanation of the symbolism here shown, translated by "The Rose" from the spirit-language :—

THE SEVEN DAYS OF CREATION.

" The seven spheres, each with a cross, represent the seven days of creation, each day with its crucifixion ; each successively created Being a suffering Being.

" The largest cross at the right hand, as looked at from the world, is the first crucifixion of God Himself in His outer individual human manifestation.

" The left cross, which is the later, and at the present time the least developed, is the mental manifestation, evolving from which is the woman's word, the outer, the inner, and the innermost. Then the cross disappears entirely, because there will then be progression without a cross. Now, in the present age, it is a progression in, and through, and with a cross.

" The whole creation is encompassed by an undeveloped triangle. The universal woman, which is represented by the large half-moon, is encompassed by the undeveloped triangle.

" The wings represent the influence of mind. We at the present time are in the sixth day, as typified by the wings attached to the sixth sphere.

" The sun with a face in it is a symbol of the whole nature of the Divine Powers uniting the undeveloped triangle to the more perfected triune of the heart. The winged heart has a cross in its upper and in its lower section, showing that the lowest as well as the highest organization must be polarized to God by crucifixion, or suffering. The spheres in each section of the heart prove that the lowest as well as the highest natures must become spherical through suffering."

I may observe, that in all the symbolic spirit drawings with which I am acquainted, whenever the crescent-moon appears it has been interpreted as the symbol of woman and progress. The triangle is perpetually used to indicate the Trinity, the three personalities of the God-power in their mystical Triune. Wings and feathers, we have been told, are typical of influence.

CHAPTER III.

LETTER FROM A FRIEND—EXPERIENCES OF A MEDIUM.

A DEAR young friend whose extraordinary Medium-ship has developed within the last thirteen months has obliged me with the following letter, which I think must have a peculiar interest in connection with the very curious drawings she has generously placed at my disposal. To her kindness I am indebted for the " Christ without Hands;" " The Bearded Christ;" " Christ among the Spheres;" " Undeveloped Spirit;" " The Woman Crucified;" " Love's Garden;" and " The Birth of Harmony."

" MY DEAR MRS. CROSLAND,

" Together with the explanation of the ' spiritual drawings' which you have chosen for your book, I think perhaps that you may find some experiences of a ' drawing medium' useful.

"People often say to me, ' Oh! it is absurd to pretend that it is not your own mind and your own will which guide your hand in these drawings. And besides, how absurd also it is of you to suppose that spirits, or "spirit," as you prefer to call it, cannot do better things in art than these imperfect sketches! You yourself, in your *common-sense* moments, draw far more correctly.' It is impossible to argue with such good friends as these, because they and 'spirit-mediums' stand upon very different planes of experience. But, for the comfort and assistance of those who are likely to enter or have already entered into the mysterious, perplexing, but after a time most sublime, experiences of this new life, it is only right, it appears to me, to chronicle one's knowledge already gained; and it is for such that I would write this letter, not for disbelievers, who can only cavil because they are utterly ignorant of something which has never yet come within their sphere of cognizance, and therefore for them is a humbug.

" Entering a foreign land where the language and the customs of its denizens are utterly unknown to him, the traveller makes many mistakes, occasionally even falling into very great dangers, and, perhaps alone through God's mercy escapes death itself. If this be the case with travellers upon the earth, is it not equally natural that there should be similar experience for the soul when it first enters into immediate and conscious communion with what in ordinary parlance is called the *invisible world?* This, spiritualists (and they are now a daily increasing and highly educated and enlightened class, and therefore worthy of credit) know from their own experiences in many ways, physical and psychical, is a thing not only possible before death, but now very frequently bestowed by God as amongst the loveliest of His gifts to His children.

" It is just a year since my hand was first guided by spirit-power to write. The discovery of this new influence dwelling within one, and softly propelling the hand to write words and sentences foreign to the ideas existing within one's own mind, must certainly be one of the most astounding moments in a human life. I know that to myself the surprise was beyond description, especially as I had been very sceptical regarding all that I had ever heard of 'spirit mediums.' It is true I had *heard* only of spiritualism and its manifestations through table-tilting, rapping, and occasionally of writing, but had never seen nor had communication with any spirit medium until this mysterious influence suddenly showed itself in our family circle, first in a younger brother, and then in myself. We had for years believed in the phenomena of mesmerism, and I immediately felt that this was a kindred phenomenon. The surprise and interest excited by the discovery it is scarcely possible to describe.

" Of the true nature and of the sacred mysteries to which the writing—or, in fact, any branch of mediumship —tends ; of its dangers, its trials, and of the laws which guide the development of spiritualism, we were all then entirely ignorant, and to this utter ignorance must be ascribed several months of most painful bewilderment and extremest distress of mind. Had we been enabled to profit by the experience of other mediums, my early initiation most probably would have been of a far less painful character ; but there must be the pioneers in all new discoveries of untrodden lands, and happy indeed those who through suffering are enabled to save others from suffering ! The first communications written thus mysteriously through my hand, and with ever-increasing physical sensations as of a most powerful mesmeric influence over my whole frame, were given, as usual, in the names of beloved departed friends and relatives, and were simple messages of affectionate greeting.

" Believing that communications proceeding from a higher state of spiritual development than that of our earth must be heavenly, pure, and true, I of course at first implicitly believed every word written by the spirit-power, believing also every word *literally*, not ever. *symbolically*.   Little were we any of us then aware that the intensest antagonism between truth and false-hood, between light and darkness, encounters the astounded and unprepared pilgrim upon his firs; entrance into the realm of spirit.   The very slightest veil but separates man in the natural world from the spiritual world which encircles him ; and when that veil is raised, as it has been occasionally by the Divine wisdom in many previous ages, even as now in our own time, the soul discovers itself surrounded by a host of new and terrible enemies, as well as by hosts cf all-powerful angelic friends.   But the language at first, even of the angelic host, is an incomprehensible mys-tery, for it is a language of symbols, which the newly-born child of spirit learns to construe only by slow and painful degrees.

" Within a fortnight of the day when spirit mediumship first came through the writing to myself, a gradual and marked change in the communications had set in. Painful messages connected with our temporal life were written, instead of those simple greetings of love from departed friends which had first arrived. At the same time with these temporal communications came also very lovely explanations of various passages in the Gospels which had always been obscure to myself, and the most earnest commands were given to pray unceasingly to Christ as the Saviour, and to trust in the Almighty's eternal ' Love, Mercy, and Peace.' The darkness was to come. Angelic Love, however, hastened to place as guides in the hands of the ignorant traveller the staff of prayer and the lamp of faith. By-and-by the messages became more and more painful, more and more temporal, and exciting in their nature, because connected with my own family circle and dearest friends. At length, written in the beloved name of a departed brother, came announcements of the approaching *deaths* of those dearest to myself, accompanied with the most painful details, and with directions for all the various medicines which would be required to ease their approaching change. My distress of mind was extreme. I believed that terrible earthly calamities were approaching for all dearest to me, and that, these calamities being so severe, this extraordinary preparation had been given, together with the assurance of the immortality of the soul and of communication between the dead and the living, as a most merciful boon from Heaven. The physical mesmerisms upon me at this period were extraordinary; I felt frequently as if enveloped in an atmosphere which sent through my whole frame warm streams of electricity in waving spirals from the crown of my head to the soles of my feet; and occasionally, generally at midnight, I was seized with twitchings and convulsive movements of my whole body, which were distressing beyond words. All these symptoms at length came to a crisis in frightful trance.

" Upon recovery from this trance, seriously ill and unutterably astounded and distressed, I willingly gave my word to my parents to cease all spirit writing. Fortunately our medical man, who was called in, had long been an earnest inquirer into spiritualism, and was a firm believer in mesmeric phenomena ; otherwise my fate might truly have been deplorable. He, though sympathetic to a certain degree, commanded me even

sternly to come out of my state of spiritual possession. I was only too anxious to free myself from the
past anguish not willingly to promise a struggle against
any relapse into the writing. My mother and I went
into the country, where, amidst sunshine, kind people
who had no interest in spiritualism, and lovely trees and
flowers, I gradually began to regain a calmer state of
mind, and my physical strength returned rapidly.
Being too much distressed at the issue of my first
experiment in spirit writing, I was not inclined to
return to it, even had I not given my solemn promise
to avoid all relapses into the mysterious experience;
and thus several weeks passed on. Soon, however, I
discovered that the mesmeric life was, though latent,
still an ever-present guest within me, a guest who
would assert his presence. My hands, either the right
or the left (for the influence affected both nearly
equally), if lying passive in my lap or upon a table or
book, would begin to be moved to write; often half a word
or a whole one, or a name, would be written before I
could stop them. I found that the tip of my finger,
placed upon a hard flat surface, would convey ideas
and sentences to my brain, as though words were

written through the finger instantaneously upon the
hard surface—I hardly knew whether I *felt* the words
or read them. Also strange knowledges regarding the
medical properties of plants and their spiritual signifi-
cations came to me if I held them or rubbed them upon
the palm of my hand—I felt as though my palms had
become clairvoyant, as, in fact, I had in an earlier stage
discovered that the region about my heart possessed the
same singular faculty when the point of my fingers
was pressed against it. The strange idea thus began
to dawn within me, that revelation of the most sacred
and spiritual knowledges can come through many other
portions of the body than those usually employed to
read printed books or even the book of nature. I began to
perceive that the fleshly tabernacle is of so wonderfully
spiritual a construction that every portion of it can reflect
the knowledge of the external world through its walls
for the edification of the indwelling soul, its guest;
whilst the soul can call forth from the invisible world
knowledges unrevealed to the ordinary senses, and pour
them through every portion of its tabernacle for their
manifestation to the external world. This was a lovely belief, and came in the train of many other beautiful ideas,

clearing away much which had always been stumbling-
blocks in my entire belief in the Scripture and the
possibility of *immediate* revelation. But pain, darkness,
and terror accompanied the light and the beauty ; and
I did not then nor until long after arrive at the
blessed assurance that antagonism is, under the Divine
command, one great means of all progression, especially
in spiritual and mental things.   These new trials came
in terrible words, referring once more to those deaths
so much dreaded by myself, being written *within my body,*
spite of my most earnest struggles against the power,
sometimes when my eyes were closed ; the words were
written in white or grey lines upon a dark ground.
I felt them within my eyelids, or upon my breast, or
within the palms of my hands,—I found my physical
organism become a mystic book upon which an unknown
most subtle and omnipotent Power could write His will.
These words would often fill me with the greatest
horror, and, to prevent their being inscribed, I have
many and many a time started up and walked rapidly
out into the fresh air, using every power of my mind
to withdraw myself entirely from the inner into the
external life, but in vain.   A power far mightier than

my own will had commenced its lovely, mysterious
work within me, and was moulding my mind and body
into that mystic organism for which we at the present
day have no other term, or perhaps dare use no
other, than 'medium of spirit.' So many of these
organisms are being developed at the present time,
that it is the bounden duty especially of medical men
to calmly and philosophically investigate the phenomena.

"Ignorance of their real nature and of their ultimate
purposes in the progress of civilization and development
of mind has already caused immense misery in many
directions, and will cause more and more, even infinitely
worse, until the time arrives that the medical world
will follow the example of Dr. Garth Wilkinson in his
valuable pamphlet on the treatment of lunacy through
spiritualism, and calmly regard this growing development, not as insanity, but as *a key whereby to unlock
insanity.* It is because in all such investigation—
investigation which is certain to come—all facts will
be useful, that I have embraced this opportunity of
slightly sketching some of the various phenomena which
have shown themselves in my own development. All

mediums would be doing a Christian service to their brethren by keeping a chronicle of their developments. Will such mediums as read this letter take to heart this suggestion, and, if they have not already done so, commence a chronicle? Such chronicles in time will be of vast importance.

" But to return to the *inward* spiritual writing. The writing development, no longer permitted to find its natural outlet through the hands, had now become *inward*. But, painful as this was, and produced by a checked effort of nature, still a fresh spiritual manifestation developed out of it—the *mediumship of drawing*. Together with the inward written words or sentences, now came single figures and groups of figures, all in outline of white or grey upon a dark ground; the explanations of which were written above their heads, beneath their feet, upon their robes, or on scrolls in the heavens, or upon the earth, on their hands, upon their swords, shields, or even sometimes as if proceeding from their lips. I could not wake in the morning without these figures instantly being drawn within my brain, over and through my heart, or within my hands. They were at once a torment and a delight—they were such a wonderful experience, so new, so awful, often of the most portentous nature, and had a character about them very much akin to Michael Angelo's creations. Three groups I especially remember:—'The Descent of the New Jerusalem' (a majestic woman clothed in wonderful draperies studded with jewels, and wearing many crowns, and a singularly beautiful breast-plate), 'The End of the World,' and 'The Last Judgment.' Also a less majestic figure painfully affected me at this time. Waking in the night, the strange drawing process instantly commenced, and I felt and saw within me the figure of an angel, whose countenance greatly resembled that of Christ, descending from a morning sky towards me, and bearing upon his shoulders a large cross, whilst from his lips proceeded these words,—'Love, Mercy, Peace; but not till after Death.' Again my soul trembled with anguish, for that strange portentous word *death* was ever written within me or without. This peculiar stage of development soon produced a singular affection of my throat, an affection of the mucous membrane, which caused several times a day, and especially when rising in the morning, the most distressing sensations. Except for this symptom I was in good physical health. After suffering thus for several days, the mysterious writing informed me that I must take a certain quantity of port-wine every day, and that then this sensation, would leave me. I followed the spiritual direction, and found almost immediate relief. About this time I took a pencil one day to make a sketch; and whilst talking to a friend who came to speak to me at the table where I was drawing, my hand rested listlessly upon. the paper before me for a minute or two. To my surprise, my hand was moved and began drawing,—*not* the design that I had had in my mind to make, but a little head, and then a very curious initial letter, like, and yet not quite like, an initial letter in some old Missal. I was surprised indeed, as I had never heard before of spiritual drawing. This surely could not bring with it pain, like the writing, nor yet bewilderment. How little did I comprehend the new class of instruction which was now awaiting me! The first drawings were very rude indeed, like the uncertain, tottering lines of a child, and also singularly resembling the designs of the very early Italian painters,—heads of Christ, angels, and curious female figures seated within spheres and hearts ; and always these drawings were accompanied with strange ornaments of spiral and shell forms, with dots and scroll-like ciphers, which I thought odd at the time, but only months afterwards, when accidentally referring to them, discovered to be the first undeveloped attempts at writing one of the 'spirit languages,' so frequently I know to be referred to in your book.

" To follow, even in the most slight and rapid manner, the history of the drawing development, would require a volume instead of a few pages. At times the power was withdrawn, and some other branch of spiritual development would take its place. Often, too, when I most earnestly desired to have a spiritual drawing given me, nothing but the merest scribble came. The fear also of the bewilderment of the spirit writing accompanied me for several months whenever I drew ; for at times my hand, whilst drawing an angel's robe, would have written through it, in curious ornament or pattern upon the drapery, words which made my soul die within me. There was always there that terrible word, *death.* At length, through God's blessing and in His own time, the key came to me. What was this word, when translated into the language of heaven, not of earth—of immortal, not *mortal*, thought? *Change!*—change of state, of life—a birth into another life! And then many words and messages began to assume other significances than those we generally assign them. And ideas of most lovely new truths gradually unfolded themselves, and old truths, breathed upon by spirit, were no longer dry bones, but clothed in the blooming freshness of immortal life. But all had to be learned through prayer, faith, love, and obedience.

" But indeed, dear friend, I have already taken up an unconscionable portion of your space, and will now leave those later spirit drawings which you have chosen for your book to speak of the peculiar kind of instruction which is conveyed through spiritual drawing, merely observing that the curious development of the internal hearing of the spirit voice was a development called forth by my dread of the spirit writing; for, after a time, that instruction which I would not receive through the *hand*, not only began to be conveyed through the internal vision in many ways, but also orally. Of the happiness and peace which gradually

K

arose within my soul after all these trials you well know, and how almost miraculous was my meeting through you with that wonderfully gifted medium, ' The Rose.' Truly she has been to us all, in our passage through the first wildernesses of spiritual experience, a rose-tree, planted there for consolation and teaching by the hand of ' Love Himself.'

" Ever, my dear Mrs. Crosland, yours,

" COMFORT."

CHAPTER IV.

CHRIST WITHOUT HANDS.—THE BEARDED CHRIST.—INSANITY AND
IDIOCY.

THE extract I am now about to make I submit to
the reader with all the reverence the nature of the
subject perforce elicits. It is a translation of the spirit
language that is found associated with the drawing
we have called " The Christ without Hands," a *fac-
simile* of which, reduced from a much larger drawing,
is herewith given. I know that CHRIST is the Greek
translation of the Hebrew word MESSIAH, both signifying " Anointed"—anointed, it may be, for the
sacrifice as well as for the ruler,—and that SHILOH
signifies " Peace-maker;" and the scholar will of
course perceive an incongruity in the use of this trinity
of terms in the following remarkable communication.
Perhaps, however, scholarly spiritualists, by elaborating
the ideas conveyed, will find a reconciling clue to any
apparent discrepancies. There is a Christian idea of
the word CHRIST very different from the Jewish

K 2

notion of MESSIAH, though philologists may choose to consider them as indicating one Personage. The idea also of " the nations" signifying the " outer, the material," is surely very suggestive. I need only remind my readers that the drawing was made through the hand of " Comfort," a narrative of whose drawing mediumship has already been given.

CHRIST WITHOUT HANDS.

" The hands and the feet represent the Outer, therefore they are here unrepresented. The Double Word is now about to be communicated, as will be seen by the writing on the place of both hands ; man's word and woman's word, the right and left of creation, the eastern and western hemispheres. The woman's word is about to come forth with power ; it will attune the countless chords of creation to one harmonious strain. The most high, the most holy, the most spiritual harmony will not yet be manifested on this earth-sphere, but, when it is once baptized with the harmonies of heaven, it will for ever respond to them. No more shall discord rule ; concord shall be the sole bond, and shall for ever enlarge and enlarge in the countless concentric

CHRIST WITHOUT HANDS

rings and circles of eternity. Then will I, who once was the Christ, come as Messiah,—Messiah, the third of which is Shiloh. First, the Saviour; secondly, the Pacificator; thirdly, the Ruler. The Jews were in error, inasmuch as they looked for the Shiloh. Firstly, I am predicated as Christ, the Suffering One; secondly, as Messiah, the Peace-maker, the Redeemer; thirdly, Shiloh, the Ruler, for then will I rule the nations with a rod of iron. The nations are the outer, the material. Spirit is the ruler, and spirits are to be the rulers in the ages that are to circle around Me. You shall walk without feet, you shall work without hands, for I will be both unto you. My Word, which has been and which is to be, shall be both unto you, even head and heart, raiment and food also. The feet, the first manifestation of power over the earth, were given in that which you received as the Books of Moses. They have passed away, they are covered now with raiment. Now My Word, My spoken Word, was dual when I was embodied on earth, because I was man and woman, male and female in one. I was a type of the first Adam, or rather a spiritual representative of him. The woman manifestation of the Divine is about to appear ; it was hidden in Me, the Christ, just as woman was hidden in man until the conditions in the outer world were ready for her reception. Now she is about to appear, be ye ready to receive ; having received her, ye shall receive Me, for we come not singly, but dual,— even more than dual, for inasmuch as the Father is with us."

The next spirit picture which, with its spirit interpretation, I shall lay before my readers, we have called "The Bearded Christ ;" and we have so named it, because, in connection with this drawing, we have been taught that there is a deep meaning in the expression "heart-shaped," as applied to the beard. I think there is a significance which spiritualists will feel in the circumstance that, simultaneously with the spread of spiritual belief and experiences in England, the manly custom of wearing the beard has been revived. Thus people who may be disposed to observe and compare different peculiarities of the beard may, with the help of the spiritual revelations which have been made on the subject, frame out an addition to the common laws of physiognomy. They may also take some interest in noticing on the pages of history how often the wearing or not wearing the beard has been associated with peculiar religious opinions or party politics. We have been told that the beard is the conductor of many beneficial spiritual influences as connected with the outer life, and therefore it has been given to Man, he being the appointed subduer of the earth. Woman, through the atmosphere of her long hair, receives that subtle influence to which allusion was made in an earlier chapter.

The spirits have instructed us to consider every beard as presenting the shape of a heart, remembering, however, that only half this shape is visible on the human countenance. A beard descending to a point from the chin has the heart-shape inward,—that is, answering somewhat to the arch of the eyebrows; while the beard which is commonly called forked has the reverse position, the invisible portion being now the point. We have been told that a beard " heart-shaped to the outer" indicates for its possessor a temperament or character that will find in the outer world the struggles and trials and purifying discipline of Life; while the pointed beard, " heart-shaped to the inner," is the sign of a nature whose conflicts will be rather those of the soul and mind than any other. It will be observed that in "The Bearded Christ" the atmosphere of the beard, as well as the beard itself, is represented; and I am acquainted with a Seeing Medium who, on many occasions, has seen the beard-atmosphere, not only when the beard is worn, but about shaven chins, with sufficient precision to decide of what shape the beard would be were it allowed to grow.

THE BEARDED CHRIST.

"I am that I am. I am He of whom it was said that He hath no form nor comeliness, because I am not and I was not of the earth, and I came unto the earth, but the earth received Me not. I was rejected, I was betrayed, I was misrepresented, I was slandered,—even more, I was crucified. I was buried, I was resuscitated, I was made evident unto woman, being the nearest approach to the spiritual; through her I was made manifest unto man in the outer; through the two, or the perfect humanity, I was enabled to show My final ascent into heaven. Earth beneath, earth-trodden, earth-corrupted, they—all peoples—were. I chose one to feed My sheep, I chose one to feed My lambs; he was

THE BEARDED CHRIST

one, the same, inasmuch as he was loving and generous, and trusted not to the outer, but to the teachings of his instincts, which are spirit teachings ; they are from the Father of Light, follow ye them.   To another in the body, in the last or the closing of the outer upon the inner world, I gave in charge the keeping of My mother. She lived seven epochs, or years, according to your calculation of time ; after that she was translated, but her spirit descended in various ways to help in the Christianizing or polarizing of the earth and its inhabitants to God.   Errors crept in and made angles in the church, until spirits appeared, who perceived and knew the true form, the angular yet spherical nature of God, which is manifested in the Word ; and He being opposed to the outer, was obliged to resist the outer, though by gentleness We did so.   I, by the telegraphic communication between the Father, His Spirit, and Myself, preserved My own oneness.   We met opponents with partial truths—not whole ones.   I was linked with God, because I was one with Him and of Him ; with man, with beasts, with vegetables, with minerals, with everything that exists in creation, because they are from and part of God—the Outer and the Inner.   By various steps and gradations, through My Apostles, I arrived at making a mark in the world : there were nine true Apostles, there were three false ones. One who should have been true was doubly false : he was doubly called, he was doubly false ; yet he was permitted to call other two, who were real Apostles. They were less true, and they were less untrue. From them radiated many, some great, many that you now call Fathers ; but, following them, many became links that united the Outer to the Spiritual World too much. The spirituality of it diminished until it became a speck ; then an effort was made, which dwindled again to a speck, only to flame up brighter. Then, in course of God's wisdom, there developed a larger power, which went on and on increasing, first of all purely for His love, but then worldly, the Outer having more than the Inner to do with the progress. Then stood at last a champion, the inner having grown very small ; being connected with the outer of the one and the inner of the other, he crucifies each, and seven great spirits are sacrificed through his ambition. Then there comes the world, the outer, that prevents any further sacrifice on his account, and a crowned horn fights against him ;

the crowned horn has eight influences,—one outer which is very large, and seven outer which are comparatively small. Then Religion goes down in the world, until it reaches and crawls upon the ground. It becomes fashionable and expedient to be religious. Occasionally you will find some one who stands up as a small hill and preaches the right, the holy, and the lofty; a prophet is seen now and then, who is rejected and trodden on by the world: unable to expand, these die, and it is only the preacher who survives and keeps his ground. Then some of them preach for the earth and point downwards: they invert their spires, they even bury them. But a time opens, the inner begins to develop; it is still below the earth, but expansion is near. Many expansions follow, until the ministers, instead of pointing downwards or upwards, point horizontally, and preach so. Then some come who aspire, and they stand like Alps crowned with snow; like the mountains and like the Alps in the outer world, they have to withstand the storm and the wind, the inward struggle and the outward temptation. Still, from their influence, many arise who will even be greater than they. Some will be greater from diving beneath, others will be greater from overshadowing them from above, from expanding above; some will give themselves a large upward bearing, so as to receive broadly the spirit of God; some will receive God at a very acute angle; they will receive of course a very small portion of Him, because the larger part of their natures is polarized to the earth. With the true Christ head and heart are equal; even in the beard you will see the type. Some are heart-shaped to the world, some to themselves; some are heart-shaped for the outer, others for the inner. Great teaching shall come through the beard and its atmosphere. I will teach truth, love, purity, faith,—all that is holy, all that is high, all that is soul-embracing, all that is mind-embracing; then with the wings of the soul and the mind I will overshadow the body; the material, the angular, and the hard shall be covered, or rather inclosed, in the marriage ring of faith. I will marry the outer to the inner, and the innermost; I will etherealize, I will spiritualize, I will mentalize My chosen, My predestined, My pre-called. They are many, they are numerous; they are more than many,—they are great. They crowd, they fill the earth, they shall fill the heavens, they shall come with banners, with flags and joyful signals; some shall come in with ensigns, and My messengers shall come with palms. The angels shall bear their crowns, for they shall be heavy with the fruit of their lives; stars, and suns, and moons, all things animate and inanimate, shall sing for joy; all creation shall be vocal, for that I the Redeemer did My work: I died not in vain, but the fruit of My labour has been gathered, bound, and housed by My prophets, My messengers, and My ministers."

I refrain from making any remarks on the more singular passages in the above communication, but give it as it was rapidly translated from the spirit language in my presence. The sort of hieroglyphic bordering to the drawing was executed only a few minutes before the translation was made, "Comfort's" hand being seized by the spirit power in my house and in my presence, and she thus compelled to add an illustration to the original drawing and writing— for illustration it is, the clue being given. The pointed horn, the eight influences, the horizontal preaching, the angular reception of God, and many other circumstances, are all clearly indicated by that rough irregular border, which was drawn by the spirit power with a rapidity only to be conceived by those who have witnessed spirit drawing.

I ought also to remark that, in allusion to the latter portion of this communication, we have been told that in the spirit symbolism a flag is considered typical of the unmarried male nature, an ensign of the single woman, and the banner is expressive of married persons. The word "lands," which occurs in the drawing, signifies "conditions."

Before closing this chapter, I will extract another translation from the spirit language. The original was written in my presence with extraordinary rapidity ; the only portion I omit was a prediction of a somewhat personal nature, the fulfilment of which commenced a few days afterwards.

INSANITY AND IDIOCY.

" Insanity is from the Inner ; Idiocy from the Innermost. Through many kinds of vicious living you might become insane and your children inherit the liability—but it would take three or four generations of vicious living to polarize them to idiocy—with some constitutions more than that. Numbers of diseases, mostly the scrofulous and the cancerous, arise from sins ancestrally conducted—insanity, theft, blindness, deafness, dumbness, when congenital, are the penalties of ancestral viciousness; inasmuch as through vicious living you polarize yourselves to the evil and not to the good spheres. You and yours become alike under the influence of darkness and evil, and your children even before their birth are interpenetrated with evil and vicious influences, and, in some instances, are incarnations of evil and demon spirits—they are even possessed before they are born. Then God frequently in His mercy, to render them saveable, makes them idiotic, so that any and every sin they do is imputed to the possessing spirit and not to them; because in the Outer they pay the penalty of transgression that in the Inner they may take their own stand and starting point. God's laws and Nature's laws are one and the same; the last are the body, the first are the soul; the regulations of man are the outer of each. Let goodness and truth walk through corruption, and impurity is not; let viciousness and evil walk through the same pathway,

and they will be doubly, triply baptized with evil
—even unto their raiment and their feet it will
attach itself. Innocence is always clothed in a suit
of chain armour—its own nature is its own protection;
viciousness is alike protected from good in a robe of
its own armour. These things will be very much
elucidated and enlarged upon by eight minds, six
male and two female, who will be made to unite and
speak as it were with one voice. . . . . . .

" Through man's being polarized to the outer and
the evil he has descended to a worse state than that
of brutehood ;—he is swineized, brutalized, and through
him woman also. In, and for, and to the outer they
both are sacrificed ; a sacrifice of corruption, the result
of which is crime and misery, insanity and idiocy,
and every kind of disease that humanity has found a
name for, and many others unknown and unnamed,
because spiritual. I will polarize Healers who shall
be bold to declare My truths, the physical, the mental
and spiritual causes of evil in all its triple forms. A
new class of medicine has been introduced, inasmuch
as it is spiritual rather than material—it is the
essence rather than the body which is administered

to the sufferer; spherical is the remedy in the outer form, which is typical of a spherical cure. The spirit only can cure—the means may lie (or be hidden) in the outer, but the spirit giveth life; because in this way wind, and earth, and water are My conductors. In them I have enshrined My life-giving and My healing powers; some are electric, some are magnetic, and some are negative. If you take a mineral, say arsenic, the smallest portion of its atmosphere becomes an electrical conductor; in that way it heals or retards recovery according to the condition of the recipient. Small as the material conductor is, the electricity conveyed is itself the conductor of a higher power. Medical men will be obliged, in fact, to be spirit healers, and to acknowledge this spirit power, and then they will be great healers; they will look upon disease and read its cause, they will touch and they will heal— My own, My commissioned ones! At present they have only one undeveloped wing, still it does aspire— this one-winged creature; if they trust to the aspiration of this wing, the other will soon expand as a balance to it. They will progress rapidly. Many now called healers are disease-imparters, inasmuch as they work for bread, and not for the love of humanity or of God. The bread shall depart from them, and it shall be given unto My own. Truly the labourer is worthy of his hire."

THE CRUCIFIED WOMAN

CHAPTER V.

THE CRUCIFIED WOMAN.—UNDEVELOPED SPIRIT.—THE SPIRIT OF
CHRIST AMONG THE SPHERES.—THE WINDOW IN THE SEPULCHRE.

THE next combination of spirit drawing and spirit
writing which is presented to the reader, we have
entitled " The Crucified Woman." From the dictation of " The Rose" I myself took down the following
translation of the spirit characters which are found
intermingled with the drawing :—

THE CRUCIFIED WOMAN.

" Woman is at present undeveloped, and therefore
crucified, because in her head is hidden a small heart of
music which responds and aspires to the great heart of
Christ. Woman's mind is polarized to Christ's heart
—Man's mind to Christ's head ; therefore she is crucified through the music of her affections, for the worldly
hand intermeddling therewith createth discord. All
sentiment, all love, will develop in this outer world
through woman's mind, and be made manifest through

woman's mind—science and knowledge through man's mind. In the ages that are to come, Developed Woman will be the great artist; for, through the fact of this aspiration in her head keeping up a telegraphic communication with the living human heart of Christ, she will be the manifester of Sacred Art. He covers her with the mantle of His influence; He is about to triunize her to the Divinity; then the whole of humanity will be vocalized by the thrilling harmonics of His vast divine love. He makes His harps, His lyres, His many-stringed instruments, and shrines them in the souls of those whom He calls to be His poets, His musicians, His artists—all that could be comprised in the Art Nature. Upon these living instruments He plays with His own fingers, with the soft, thrilling fingers of His lightnings, the reverberating notes of His thunders, His roaring, surging seas, His cataracts, His thundering avalanches, His mighty winds, His soft, sighing, playful zephyrs. These outer things are all the influences emanating from His different fingers, and He has now struck the key-notes in many hearts. He has attuned some to the heavenly concords; others are being attuned. When His orchestra is filled and attuned, the burst of melody that will descend upon the

UNDEVELOPED SPIRIT

earth will baptize the whole earthly creation: your aged and your young, the old man and the babe, will alike breathe an atmosphere of music and of love, and nature will be vocal to them, because within their spirits the harmonies of heaven will for ever thrill, and sound, and swell, and echo."

"Undeveloped Spirit" is the appropriate title given to a spirit drawing which, at the first glance, bears some resemblance to the mediæval designs with which antiquarians are familiar. Written on the trefoil leaf, which, we have been told, ought to have been drawn still more resembling a Winged Eye, are spirit characters which have been thus translated:—

"Until My Second Eye is seen, Spirit will not develope. Man is developed to the utmost in the outer; God's male Eye has been opened to man; God will now commence manifesting unto both man and woman the Female Eye of His Providence. Then spirit will develope. As yet, in man's sight, the female eye of the Divine Providence is unformed, almost unknown. Divine Spirit, revealed to man through woman's nature, will soon commence its work of regeneration. Spirit of woman, polarized to God, shall soar, shall work, shall achieve."

Upon the breast of the figure of Humanity is written : " Science shall fail, Religion shall fail, until both are polarized to the Two Eyes of God."

Upon the spirit figure,—upon the vesture which shall be rent, which is already falling, is written : " When the veil is torn, progression shall commence. Feet shall be liberated ; but even then the spirit form will be undeveloped. It will have feet ; it will stand. It is now held, because the time is not yet ready for its palpable progress."

I have now to introduce two spirit drawings, concerning which there are some singular characteristics. But as " Comfort" has kindly favoured me with the precise account of the manner of their production, I gladly avail myself of her graphic description :—

THE SPIRIT OF CHRIST AMONG THE SPHERES.

"*April*, 1857.—The origin of this drawing is curious. About three months ago my drawing mediumship was entirely removed for two months, during which time I had only 'spirit language' written through my hand. The very day that I had the power of spiritual drawing first withheld, I took out the cardboard upon which there now is this sketch of Christ amongst the spheres. I had been thinking that a lovely design might be made from the old legend of the Virgin Mary being fed by angels, when a child, in the Temple ; and I hoped that I might have this design given me as a ' spirit drawing.'

"I found, however, that, instead of the figure of the happy little ' Virgin,' as I expected, a figure of a child with a most agonized expression of countenance was represented. A network of prison bars was drawn over the child, as though she were seated in a cage. A figure of a very stern angel was also sketched in, in the place now occupied by the symbol of Christ's spirit. The outstretched hand of the angel was represented as if locking the cage-door, and then his face was drawn turning away from the child in prison. I could obtain nothing more except that beneath the child's feet was written ' *Thyself: thy prison-door will not yet be opened.*' Also a mask expressive of great sternness, and almost cruelty, was drawn as if placed before the angel's head, but looking in the direction of the prison. The figure of the child in its prison was sketched in the space now occupied by the curious symbol of the winged woman's head in the sphere to the right hand of Christ's symbol. I was greatly distressed at this and wept very much. Two months followed, not only of withdrawal of my artistic mediumship, but of severe trial in many ways.

"About a month ago, remembering this curious sketch of the imprisoned child and the angel, which I had not looked at since the day it was made, I brought it out, and my drawing mediumship having just faintly returned, I thought I would pray whether I might be allowed to work upon it once more, trusting now that the prison-door would be unlocked.

"To my great joy my hand was freely moved, and the angel turned into a figure of Christ, or rather I ought to say a symbol of Christ, for these drawings are but as yet rude hieroglyphics. Then the four spheres were sketched in, producing a kind of cross with rounded ends, a very favourite symbol in all the sketches given me, and, I am told, typical of this new outpouring of spirit power in the world. May it not also signify that there is a peculiar *sphere* of suffering *belonging to each end of the cross?*

CHRIST AMONG THE SPHERES

" Within the largest sphere, above the floating figure of Christ, were written also in smaller spheres the words ' God' and the ' Holy Ghost,' and the sphere or halo around Christ's head was surrounded by twelve still smaller spheres. The child seated in its prison was entirely rubbed out, except its head, which, with its agonized expression, was still left. Two other heads were added to this head, one on each side ; all three as if proceeding from one neck, and all most unhappy-looking. Beneath these heads was written, ' UN-DEVELOPED STATES OF WOMAN—*Insanity, disease, and disbelief : for these three evils Christ is the mighty Healer.*' The outstretched hand of Christ was now drawn more perfectly, and as if touching the large sphere which surrounded the three heads; the hand was represented pointing with the two fingers and thumb. Upon this the middle head had a body added to it, that of an undraped and sleeping Eve ; the head belonging to the body was altered and made to correspond with the sleeping figure, whilst the two remaining heads glared over the reposing figure like demons. Now these two heads were removed ; not, however, before the rubber held in my hand had been moved to touch the hand of Christ, and from His hand was moved over the paper to the demon-heads. The eyes of Eve were then opened with an astonished gaze, and her lips touched so as to make a vague smile come into her countenance. The next change was that the figure of Eve was clothed. A veil first wrapped over her head, and then garments which assumed the character of Egyptian drapery, and beneath the feet were written the words, ' *Changes in Woman's Spiritual and Natural State.*' A sort of Gothic or mediæval costume next developed itself out of the Egyptian, followed by the dress of some half-dozen different eras, and ending with that of the present day, the little cap perched at the back of the head being represented by a large butterfly. When Eve had reached this stage, the entire sphere was cleared with bread and India-rubber, and a much larger head was drawn, as if emerging out of a chrysalis. At first a butterfly perched upon the woman's brow; then she herself seemed to become a butterfly, for large gauzy wings were drawn springing forth from her shoulders; her arms, however, still remained undeveloped, unreleased out of her imprisoning chrysalis.

" The head of Christ also underwent many changes

at this stage of the sketch, and His figure also, the figure being sometimes drawn like that of a woman, and the countenance being represented without a beard. I asked why these curious changes took place in this symbol of our Lord, and also why the drawing was still so imperfect. And the inward voice informed me that 'our Lord would reveal Himself to the world now through spiritualism, as the Bride as well as the Bridegroom; and that, therefore, in the symbols about to be given forth of Himself in art, He would be constantly represented as uniting the *two* characters of this mystic and glorious union promised in the New Jerusalem; also, that the reason why Christ's head so frequently altered its character was because the ideal of Christ in the human soul altered and developed just as the spheres of the soul developed; and, as regarded the imperfection of the drawing, that that was only a type of my own imperfection as a medium, and of the imperfect development of spiritual knowledge and power in general.' I was also told to observe the imperfect outline of the spheres, and to regard this imperfection as proceeding from the fact that our knowledge was not yet perfected in any one sphere of God's love.

"After these changes in the figure of our Saviour had been completed to the point at which they now appear in the sketch, a lily and a palm branch were placed in His left hand, and behind them, within the left sphere, the figure of a mother was drawn, with a child lying upon her lap. These figures are still very imperfect; but I was told to leave them in their imperfection, as this very imperfection was typical of the present state of spiritualism; that is to say, when the spirit child is but just born on the earth, and has only as yet been kissed by the most undeveloped symbol of Heaven—a little cherub. Many very curious things were communicated regarding this sphere, which was called ' the sphere of the Spirit Mother,' but it would occupy too much space here to write them all down.

" In the lowest sphere of all, over which Christ's raiment floats, at first very roughly, a bowed female figure was sketched, and out of this figure developed the odd mass of symbols now seen in the drawing. The whole resembles a *burst shell*, filled with types of Death which are evolving into Life. This part of the drawing was given at Easter. I had no clear explanation with it, but was told that ' The Rose' had the key to it, all the forms being ciphers in the spirit language, written through me and interpreted by her. These symbols are evidently typical of Life coming forth out of Death; Death, according to all spiritual teaching, being but another name for Birth, the passing out of one stage of existence into another, one of the forms of progression.

"I would willingly have made the whole of this drawing much more perfected artistically, but have not been permitted. When the head of the symbolic woman with wings had been crowned with grapes and corn, the name of God in the upper sphere was re-written, the small spheres which formed the word becoming partially heart and partially kernel-shaped. I ought also to observe that a large serpent had been sketched during the progress of the drawing, around the 'sphere of woman,' and behind Christ's figure, but was gradually obliterated by the dark shading behind the spheres, and I was told 'that the Serpent would be annihilated when the Bride and the Bridegroom should become one.'

"'The Rose,' when she saw this drawing, told me that the twelve small spheres surrounding the head of our Saviour represen tthe Tribes of Israel. She can explain to you the *innermost* meaning of the drawing. I have only given what came to me, the ' *outermost of the inner.*' "

" Love's Garden," or " The Window in the Sepulchre," as the next spirit picture has been called, presents another instance of spirit teaching coming through a succession of symbolic designs :—

THE WINDOW IN THE SEPULCHRE.

" *Good Friday*, 1857.—This morning having read chapter xx. of St. John, I prayed that I might be permitted to make a drawing of Christ's appearance to Mary Magdalene in the garden after His resurrection. The drawing was given me, but not treated, as I expected, as a picture, but rather as a page of hieroglyphics. The wall of the sepulchre is represented behind our Lord, whilst Mary, turning towards Him, stands at the mouth of the sepulchre. This wall is inscribed with hieroglyphics, and is in fact a missal-page, written over with spirit symbols. The vine which clusters over it, and from the branches of which rich clusters of grapes depend, is not a naturalistic drawing of a vine, but given as a symbol of the 'True Vine.' Its stem resembles both a scaly serpent and the trunk of a palm-tree, and rises from shell-like forms—all ciphers of the spirit language, which 'The Rose' interprets.

"The inner voice told me whilst my hand drew, that 'this represented the tree of life, the tree of tradition, the tree of human progress; and that the two feather-like forms springing from its foot, but beneath the branches of the vine, were types of the Adam-and-Eve-life; whilst the vine itself was a type of the Christ-life, the perfected and over-shadowing vine.'

"Behind the figure of our Lord, and seen beyond the corner of the wall of the sepulchre, is a mystic portal. It is carved over with the Runes of the spirit language, forming strange dragon-like architectural decorations. This portal is guarded by a mystic beast, with a bird's head, a dragon's wing, and a huge eye in the centre of its serpent coil. Two rolled-up mummies are seen within the portal, one leaning against the other as if for support. Spirit language is written above and around them. The voice said within me, 'This is a house of much woe, the house of Egyptian darkness.

Within it dwells the true death. There the Redeemer, the life and light-giver, hath not entered. To that house the voice of the living God hath not penetrated. The ears of the mummies are stuffed with the dust of the earth. Their noses cannot scent the spring, nor yet their lips utter truth and life. But the Saviour approaches, His dear feet hasten to their deliverance, His dear voice commands the unrolling of their swaddling-clothes of death, and their eyes shall be opened, and their lips praise the Sun of the universe.'

" Christ's figure was again and again clothed in different garments, over which different patterns were drawn, all in forms of the spirit language. His hands also were drawn in different positions, sometimes raised as if in benediction, sometimes stretched forth towards the figure of Mary who stands at the entrance of the sepulchre. Her figure and garments also underwent various changes. Sometimes, I was told, she represented Mary the Magdalene, type of deepest love, of deepest degradation, of deepest suffering, of deepest repentance. Sometimes she was her sister Martha, sometimes she was the spirit of all humanity, sometimes

THE WINDOW IN THE SEPULCHRE

a type of the medium nature in general, and of my whole soul in particular.

" At length when a palm-branch and lily were placed in the left hand of our Lord, the countenance and form of Mary became more perfected, and her lips parted with a smile. She recognized the Lord, and her soul sang allegiance to the ' Heavenly Bridegroom.'

" On Easter Monday I prayed that I might be permitted to draw the two angels within the sepulchre. Their figures were immediately given me, but sketched in so imperfectly that I felt they were there only temporarily, and as a means of imparting instruction. Their two heads were united in a sphere, and I was told by the inward voice, ' that if in the house of woe, the house of Egyptian darkness, the mummies were united in the sphere of sympathy, much more should I find that the blessed and angels were united in a sphere of sympathy and labour.' Then the angels had masks of great pain and ugliness drawn over their faces, and the words were written beneath these masks—' Masks of devils : in other words, masks of Satan, the angel of trial and temptation. A mask of fear of man, and a mask of the fear of insanity.' Then these masks were

M

rubbed out, and one angel was drawn in place of the two, a very imperfect angel indeed, and beneath her feet was written 'Woman.' This figure was clothed in various strange garments. It was as though a butterfly's wings were made to clothe her, and these various wings formed different styles of costume; as for instance, the wings placed on either side of the head formed a kind of Mary Queen of Scots head-dress; placed upon the shoulders a Queen Elizabeth's ruff; upon the hips the hoop of Queen Anne's reign. The words 'Butterflies of various ages' were written beneath the figure. The angel, or woman, or butterfly, was entirely rubbed out, and a huge rose-shaped window was drawn in place of the figure, and the voice told me that this was a window of love, through which God's light should stream, to illumine the gloom of woman's sepulchre; that Mary the Magdalene, and Martha also, had just gone forth from the sepulchre, having found their Lord arisen, and were listening to His words of life, but that many women were still asleep in the tomb with the cast-off garments of their Saviour, but that the light through this window should arouse them, and they also should arise and go forth with glad tidings in their hearts to join the band of the living led onward by their Lord 'into ever progressive wisdom and truth.'

" The window now lost its appearance of a rose and assumed a singular aspect, that of a Chinese lantern, from which depended two peculiar forms. They appeared to me two fruits shaped somewhat like figs. The sepulchre was shaded by my hand, of course guided mesmerically, and as the delicate shading slowly proceeded, the words were spoken through my brain by the inner voice. 'Coming events cast their shadows before them.' The fig-like fruits assumed a more developed aspect; they were a pair of lutes depending from the lantern, and between them hung the martyr's palm. The whole form resembled a strange balloon. I thought to myself 'A balloon? that is not by any means an agreeable symbol!' The inner voice said to me in reply, 'Does not spiritualism, when only awakening out of its tomb, present to the eyes of Egyptian blindness a form as of a balloon, a silly, vain, presumptuous, and highly dangerous mode of progression? Be satisfied. To the externally-minded it is a balloon, to the internally-minded it is a pair of lutes proceeding from a sphere of light and united by the martyr's palm.

" I now thought, ' But still the two angels have not been drawn in the sepulchre ? '

" The voice inwardly asked me, as if in reply to this question,—

" ' What *are* angels ? '

" ' Messengers from God,' I returned in thought.

" ' And are not words sent by God, messengers ? ' continued the inner voice. ' And what are symbols but words ? ' it pursued—' words sent to teach divine truths ? Such words or symbols are messengers from God, therefore angels. Thou hast had thy angels drawn for thee in the sepulchre.'

" *April* 21*st*, 1857.—The shading in the sepulchre having been completed very carefully, my hand was moved to take bread and entirely cleanse a space in the centre of the blackness, the voice saying within me : ' When the darkness is quite developed, then is the end of the darkness, and then commences the light. And, if it be the will of God, where has been the greatest darkness, the greatest deadness, there shall arise the strongest light and life. *Spain ! Spain !* ' repeated the voice very emphatically. Fearing that this word ' Spain ' might be spoken by a spirit of undevelopment and evil, interrupting the communication, I prayed earnestly that the evil might be removed. The voice, however, still continued to repeat ‘Spain ! Spain ! ’ and then, whilst my hand was moved to sketch in roughly the form of a window within the cleansed place, the voice pursued as follows :—

“ ‘ This window typifies that window which the Lord is opening in the souls of the spiritual-minded, the window of truth and of light, through which Divine wisdom and love shall flow into the new church of the New Jerusalem, the church of the Lamb of God. Read with reverence and adoration the truths which angelic spirit-fingers shall trace in symbols upon this window ; symbols rude at first, but gradually growing towards beauty as the spiritual and physical being of humanity becomes educated for the service of the Divine Instructor. This window is a mingling of rude and imperfect hieroglyphics, because the soul and the hand of the human medium employed are those of one but just born into the spiritual kingdom. Learn that *gradual growth*, that development of the perfect out of the imperfect, of light and order out of chaos, is the law of Divine creation in the spiritual as well as in the natural spheres of being. Intellect is not matured in a day nor yet in a year; neither is spirit matured in a day nor yet in a year. Spirit is the twin of intellect, the sister whose existence has not yet been generally recognized by the world, although her being is co-existent with intellect in the nature of humanity. In these latter ages the world has alone paid homage to intellect, the *male* genius implanted by God in humanity. The female genius, spirit, the latest of the twins manifested by God in the dual soul of His human children, will now, slowly and unexpectedly, be revealed by the Divine command, throughout the world, to such as are willing and prepared to receive her.

"'This window is a type of the dual nature of the human soul with its male and female natures, both equally undeveloped as yet,—the one developed most to the external world, the other most to the internal; yet neither perfected in either direction. Arrived now, however, at an equal point of partial development, intellect and spirit are about to be united in an indissoluble union for an eternal progression towards God's innermost temple of love and wisdom.

"'The light from the realm of love and wisdom, con-

veyed through the window of combined spirit and intellect, will arouse the sleepers in the sepulchre of Europe,
and thus celestial light shall awaken even Spain, that
nation of all Europe most deeply sunk into lethargy.
The soul of Spain sleeps a long sleep of death—sleeps
but for a time, but for an age—sleeps but to restore
her exhausted energies. Aroused by the outpouring of
spirit and of truth, her ancient vigour will revive,
purified and developed into a higher life. The blacker
the evil, the coarser and narrower the prisons in which
Satanic forces have bound her soul, the more wondrous
the Divine miracles which shall be manifested in the
ages of her awakening in the spirit, in the intellect, and
in the body.

" ' Italy is nearer to a revival of life and of truth. But
hers is not yet the spiritual awakening. Hers is the
mental awakening. A mental awakening in former
ages was the forerunner of her decay in literature and
in art. The *renaissance* of mind was the birth of
scepticism as regards the invisible, but ever active and
most subtle, influences of spirit; and faithless men
became the decaying imitators of an art-world, the
creator of which had been Divine Spirit flowing through

obedient and faithful human beings. The revival of art and literature in Italy is not yet. Their revival in fullest fulness is alone to come when spiritual art is completely developed in the world. Then will her new and grandest Michaels and Raphaels arise and become the earthly archangels of art; for Italy is the mother of art-nations, and will once more become the world's art-instructress through her inspired children. But first must her mental revival be completed; this time the precursor of faith in the invisible, not as formerly the precursor of what in spiritual language is called *death* or infidelity. In Spain, however, the first revival will be spiritual rather than mental, for hath not the world long read that "the first shall be last, and the last first"?

"'This is the window of truth and of light: "The last shall be first, and the first shall be last." Where there has been most earthly oppression, there shall be the most heavenly consolation. Upon the Negro, upon the Hindoo, upon the South-Sea-Islander, shall stream light through this heavenly window. The Divine is the Father, the Mother, the Lover, the Cherisher of His peoples. His Son, in this His inner manifestation of His presence upon earth, through His innumerable faithful ones, through His heavenly and earthly messengers, through His heavenly and His earthly voices, His harmonies of spiritual and natural natures, through His thunders, His winds, His flowers, His stars, His symbols, animate and inanimate, will cleanse His world of its Satanic foes. He will develop, will perfect, will crown with His blessings of LOVE, MERCY, PEACE.

"'This is the window of truth and of light; this is the window of spirit. Upon the whole social and political life of the earth will Spirit cast her radiance, and then first truly will the world's history be written. Then from the ashes of traditions now dead and grey, kindled into new life and flame by the spiritual beams of Love and Truth, will the true history of the world, new yet ever old, arise, the veritable Phœnix! Symbols of the inner and the innermost, traced in hieroglyphics by the hands of the most ancient peoples, illumined by light from the temple of the Lamb, will praise the Eternal, the Omnipresent, the Omnipotent Poet of the universe, with their myriad unsealed lips. Heraldry even, that dead signal of the most external life of the present day, will then first receive its crown of beauty and its legend of significance, for spiritual light will illumine its blazonments, will decipher its mediæval hieroglyphics, and, yet more, will create a fresh heraldry for higher and holier purposes. Of mechanism, of astronomy, of botany, of natural history, of chemistry, of electricity, of photography, of physiology, of all creation, animate and inanimate, will spirit teach new wonders and lovelinesses, and guide humanity along their varied paths into the highest and holiest knowledges. All creation shall resound with praise to its Creator, uttered in voices yet unrevealed !

" ' I AM THE TRUTH AND THE LIFE. I AM THE LIGHT. I AM THE WINDOW OF HEAVEN,' speaks the voice of Christ. ' I AM THE BEGINNING AND THE END. Windows shall be opened in MY names of Wisdom and of Love. For earth, as long since promised by Myself, shall have intercourse with heaven. Simplest children will I choose to unfold My truths ; simplest women untaught by the earthly schools. Let My words be revered as truth and light. Let man treat My messengers with mercy and with love, even as man desires My angels to watch over him with love and with mercy. Amen.' "

CHAPTER VI.

DISCOURSE ON THE TRINITY RECEIVED THROUGH THE ALPHABET
BY RAPS.—THE OFFERINGS OF THE MAGI.—AN INSPIRATION.

IT has been said by disbelievers in modern spiritual
manifestations, that the supposed communications, as
they call them, from the spiritual world never transcend the intelligence of human beings, and are often
indeed of an extremely trivial or even ridiculous
character. In answer to such objections I may
observe, that if these communications did completely
transcend the power of our understanding, they would
of necessity be incomprehensible, and consequently
valueless; while I leave it to the candid judgment of
my readers to decide whether the specimens of spiritual communications which I have already presented
and am about to offer, do or do not, in the majority
of instances, quite touch the highest point of sublimity which the popular mind is prepared to comprehend or appreciate.

That many of the stories concerning spiritual manifestations which have been current in newspapers and periodicals present a painful amount of profanity and puerility, I am as ready to admit as the staunchest anti-spiritualist can be to assert. But what does this fact prove? Only that by the law of affinity like attracts like, and that if persons are so light-minded and irreverent as to use the gift of mediumship for merely the idle purpose of eliciting the wonderful, and put themselves in the way of receiving manifestations without prayer, and without solemnity of heart, they will assuredly by their frame of mind—by the condition of their personal spiritual atmospheres—drive far away the angelic hosts whose mission is to guard, to teach, and to purify, and at the same time will attract " undeveloped spirits, ' who appear to delight in cheating and misleading human beings.

Again, from the strange questions which persons inclined to believe in the manifestations often first put to the spirits, it would really seem that they suppose disembodied spirits to be omniscient ; forgetting that the whole universe is made up of the servants of GOD, each of whom moves in a prescribed orbit. Our own Guardian Angels and Ministering Spirits can generally tell us all that it behoves us to know; but it does not follow that they are acquainted with the affairs of strangers. And here I may observe, that by Guardian Angels I mean God-given guides, intelligences who have never been embodied on earth; and by Ministering Spirits are understood the beatified dead who have either known and loved us on earth, or are attracted to help us on our life-journey through some subtle affinity of nature or character.

Let me illustrate what I mean by ministering spirits. A seeing medium, to whom allusion has already been made in these pages, once passed an evening in the company of the late Duke of Wellington. She was little more than a child at the time, but she had been a seeress from the period of her earliest recollection—fancying, when four years old, that fairies had come to play with her—and, as was her wont, perceived on this occasion a throng of spirits moving about among the human company. Near the Duke,—evidently one of his ministering spirits, in close affinity with him, and well accustomed to act through his sapphire-blue atmosphere,—was a majestic female figure; and while the seeress was pondering in her own mind whether it might be mother or wife who was thus ministering to the Duke, she tells me there were written above the head of the spirit in letters of flame the words "Elizabeth of England."

Is this a story to laugh at? I think not. To me it lets in a wonderful light on God's Providence, and suggests a grand idea of His mighty scheme for the world's progress. It has been said that the dead still "rule our spirits from their urns;" but if it could be generally realized that the Spirits of the Just made Perfect find part of their beatitude in carrying out God's purposes, still basking in the light of His countenance, though descending to help their fellowmen; that Heaven, instead of being a place of selfish rest far removed from human interests, presents conditions of happy activity and endless progress,—I think many a careless liver would be urged towards amendment, and cheered forward by bright hopes, and at the same time ardent desires for his own instant regeneration. There is warrant in Scripture for this faith, the faith that the departed do appear on earth in a guise that is recognizable. Witness the appearance of Moses and Elias talking with our Lord.

Let me repeat that all we have been taught concerning the laws of the spiritual world tends to show that disembodied spirits are attracted to us while we are still embodied by a principle of affinity ; and that the greater degree of elevation and purity our own souls attain, the holier will be the nature of those ministering spirits who are sent to help us. Does not this fact, if it once be acknowledged as a fact, give a new meaning to the words of our Lord, " Unto every one that hath shall be given, and he shall have abundance ; but from him that hath not shall be taken away even that which he hath " ?

If, therefore, people seek spiritual manifestations merely from a desire to witness the wonderful ; if they ask silly, worldly questions, instead of reverentially, and with prayer to be defended from evil, awaiting the manifestations which may be vouchsafed, they will, in all probability, be misled or deluded, or receive communications of so puerile a character, that the occasion and the privileges, which ought to be considered solemn, will appear profane or ridiculous. But that communications of a sublime character may be made through the much-scorned method of the raps, the following discourse will, I think, testify :—

DISCOURSE ON THE TRINITY RECEIVED THROUGH THE ALPHABET BY RAPS.

" God the everlasting Father and His co-eternal Son the Christ are indeed one and the same Being, God the Incomprehensible.

" But the Holy Ghost, the Spirit of love and truth, is an influence or emanation proceeding from the Father and the Son, pervading all space continually and for ever proceeding from the one God, and acting on the souls of all men.

" By the influence of the Holy Spirit the angels themselves are upheld in righteousness. And thus God does indeed reveal Himself to His universe as Father, Son, and Holy Spirit.

" As light from the sun so the Holy Spirit floweth from the Lord God.

" Who can discern, who can imagine the love of God the Redeemer ?

" Having chosen to suffer for the sins of His

creatures, His sufferings were, like His attributes, infinite and incomprehensible.

" All creatures in the universe, high and low, if united in one body, could not have borne that weight of woe.

" He suffered for the sins of all worlds, wherever His erring creatures were scattered, and this He told us when He said : ' And other sheep I have which are not of this fold.'

" All goodness is of God. He is the one Fountain whence all love, truth, and wisdom for ever flow. No creature hath any merit of his own ; all that the most exalted angels have, they received and yet receive continually of God.

" But God is pleased to impute merit to His servants. He rewards the virtues which Himself inspires. Jesus Christ, the Lord of Glory, is the cause of all real happiness — the giver of all love, friendship, and affection, all kind and generous feelings. If there be any holy joy, Jesus is the cause. All evil is of Satan, but in Christ is plenteous redemption.

" It was not the number of the transgressors that moved the Almighty to compassion, for the Lord Jesus would have suffered and died to save but one immortal soul from misery, so great, so wonderful is the love of our Redeemer.   Who can describe—who can imagine— the agonies of a suffering God?   Having chosen to suffer for the sins of His creatures, His sufferings were infinite.

" All creatures are or have been sinners, therefore the Lord Jesus took upon Himself the sins of a whole universe; being omnipresent and almighty, He suffered for sin in all worlds at one and the same time. Thus Christ has exhibited the profound depth of infinite love.   No other way of pardon could have moved man to so ardent a return of love.   No other way of reconciliation could have so well shown forth the holiness of God, and His hatred of all sin.

" No other scheme of Providence could so wonderfully and so beautifully have displayed the love of God.   In a word, man's Redemption by Jesus Christ the Righteous exhibits all the attributes of God in full perfection, and will for ever move the hearts of an adoring universe.

" The hearts of saints and angels as they look on Christ will for ever burn with ardent gratitude, and for ever glow more and more intensely with a flame of holy love.

" Christ's whole life on earth was one continued scene of pain and sorrow. He was the Man of sorrows, so styled in dread pre-eminence.

" He, for our sakes and for our transgressions, unrobed Him of His glory, to live the life and die the death of man.

" Yet He was still the mighty God, the Prince of life, the sovereign Lord of the universe, the unfathomable and mysterious One. He hath said of Himself, ' I am that I am.' For ever and for ever He will still be wonderful and alone.

" He is thus the Redeemer as well as the Creator of a universe. Give, then, as the royal David exclaims, ' Give unto the Lord the glory due unto His name, worship the Lord in the beauty of holiness! '

" The Lord Christ is seen in the form of man in heaven ; but there is a glorious light around Him. He is the Lord of Glory.

" None can see the Father but by looking on the Son.

" It was the substantial part of God, the glorified and eternal body of Christ, called the Son of God which took flesh and dwelt with men on earth, not the spiritual essence or soul of Jehovah.

" Yet the Father dwells in Christ, and Christ in Him : they are inseparable. No man hath seen Jehovah at any time. He is unfathomable, eternal, invisible, mysterious, wonderful, and incomprehensible ! Yet hath He revealed Himself to men in the person of His eternal Son ;—and God and Christ are one. They are one and the same Being, and can never be divided. And as is His majesty so is His mercy. The Holy Ghost is an influence proceeding from God and Christ—from the Father and the Son—from the soul and body of God—from the eternal essence and the eternal substance. The Holy Spirit therefore dwelt in Christ while He was upon the earth, and kept the Father and Son united ; yet the eternal essence of Deity remained unobscured and undefiled — the life and light of the universe, dwelling in the light which no man can approach unto.

" How God the Father could thus separate His essence from His substance is even to us, His angels and ministering spirits, a mystery.

" Christ alone can comprehend the Father ; and the

everlasting Father reveals Himself to His creatures through the Christ.

" The body of Christ is substantial and eternal ; so also is the spiritual essence of God, which is God the Father. Yet is this essence beyond conception pure, and different from all substance. All nature exists but in God. He made all that is. God is the only absolute and real existence. All other beings have derived all their powers from Him, and still exist in Him and through Him.

" The Lord is from everlasting to everlasting, and He reigneth for ever and ever. By His will He made all worlds. He spake and the universe was created. All things sprang to life and light at His sovereign word. All in heaven bow down in adoration of the Lamb that was slain ! "

The following extract from the journal of our circle needs no comment. The communication was made in the presence of a lady and a gentleman with whom I am well acquainted, and whose excellent sense and integrity are esteemed by all who know them. The medium was in a spirit or mesmeric trance at the time of the occurrence mentioned :—

THE OFFERINGS OF THE MAGI.

" We had been speaking of the nativity of Our Lord, and especially of the three wise men from the East and their several offerings. We thought that there was a deep symbolism in them, which had never yet been explained. While we were still speaking on the subject, a spirit came, of a very venerable and majestic aspect, and made the following communication :—

" ' I am one of the three who witnessed the first manifestation of the God-power in the Outer. I was attracted to you by your conversation, and am polarized to you through it. Our three offerings—the gold, the frankincense, and the myrrh—represent the three comings of God to His creatures. These are also symbols of body, mind, and spirit ; the first has now passed away. We followed His star, because not a leaf grew and faded, not a bird swept its wings through the air, not a living creature dragged itself on the earth, but to us were types of ideas that had been and passed away, or prophecies of those that were to come.

" ' The cause of the fall of Egypt and Chaldæa, under God's Providence, was, that their inhabitants were disposed to worship the organization itself rather than the spirit which caused that organization. They acknowledged the spirit, but the outer was too strong for them. This you will see shown in the custom of embalming the dead. And then to the Jews for a time was given the mental or religious rule of the East, according to the wiseness and foreknowing power of God. They persisted in adhering to one old idea, rejecting all new ; hence they conserved as much as they received, and sometimes perverted. God then had to call another people to receive and acknowledge His first manifestation in the world, and this is typified by the Chaldæan three. Three nations will be called of God to show forth His three manifestations. England will be the last commissioned, because it will represent the spirit. The mind you will receive from America, because the first idea came in the extreme East with the rising sun, and when that idea had rolled itself to the extreme West, there was born the frankincense mani-festation, the mind manifestation from the grave. Thus will be formed an earthly triangle. To England will come the manifestation of the Shiloh. He will come to England as the Bridegroom with the Bride, and to the

Anglo-Saxon race the rule will be given. England will be the last, because she is comprehensive, she is all-embracing. Her colonies and provinces dot the globe, because the English spirit is the most universal on earth. Resulting from that spirit, the English language will be the most universal, because it can be made to expand and embrace all other languages. Therefore, when the curse is removed that came in the childhood of man, it will be the bond of union, and the marriage ring of nations. God chose His first people from the most degraded and outer-minded of nations, because through them came His lowest and most outer manifestation.

" 'He has chosen America, because many puritanical spirits were sent thither ; and He has made His mind to be manifested there. They were of a higher nature than the first ; they were persecutors, and persecuted of a higher power. They too were strong in prejudices.

" 'He has chosen England and the English people for the highest manifestation of His power, because England is naturally recipient of all nations. This is to show that His mission is to all. Also, He has chosen the English people because the individual atoms constituting the nation are more spherical, have greater liberty, and are more insular than any other people. This is to show that all must be insular and spherical before God can be in them and act through them, and the three God-powers dwell for ever with them.'

" He then intimated that the subject would be resumed on another occasion, because there was neither time nor strength for its immediate completion."

The next extract, and with which I shall close this chapter, has been called " An Inspiration." The medium through whom it was given assures me that she did not know one sentence before another what was coming. She describes her sensations while she was compelled to write this paper as resembling the listening to a sound of gushing waters, which yet took an articulate voice. I am personally and intimately acquainted with three mediums who are accustomed to receive sublime communications through the "inner voice :"—

AN INSPIRATION.

" The angels see the external glory of God the Father ; but they can only catch occasional glimpses of His internal glory through the face of the Son.

" But the pure spirit or deep soul of God is unnamed and unknown by man ; the first shining forth of this God-power will bring in a new dispensation, and the Almighty Father will then reveal Himself to His children as an Almighty Mother.

" Then shall the church and the woman sing for joy ; God-commissioned shall the Church then be arrayed in power. She shall rule the whole earth. All government shall be given unto her, and reside for ever in her ; not in her members, but in the church only and entirely.

" Then also shall woman rejoice, for the dawn of her Easter will be seen and felt by the aching head and throbbing heart of humanity.

" The angels sang for joy when God was born into the outer world of man. All angels and men, all beings celestial and terrestrial, shall sing for joy at this inner spiritual birth of God that is to be in the most holy, most celestial sphere. Then shall the woman's word be revealed ; dowered with love, clothed with beauty, it shall be written, it shall be spoken.

" Even as the woman was the completion of man, so shall the woman's *word* be the completion of the man's *word.*

" Though man and woman are two, yet they are one humanity ; and though the man's word and the wo- man's word are 'two, yet they are one word. And the union of these two words shall give birth to a spirit power that shall rule all flesh. Then shall Shiloh appear."

CHAPTER VII.

SPIRIT EMBLEMS.—SYMBOLS.

It is now my task to describe a phase of Spiritualism which, to those who are best acquainted with it, is only second in interest to the writing and interpretation of the spirit language. Within the last few months, the young lady, the seeing medium to whom I alluded at page 34, has been shown certain Spirit Emblems, and instructed that they belong to certain specific individuals, and are to be associated with such personages as symbols alike of their inner lives and outward actions. I am well aware that a mere assertion of this sort from a single nameless seeress is not likely to carry conviction to the reader, unless supported by other evidence ; and, therefore, though I know her to be as little likely to prove the victim of deception as she is to be herself a deceiver, it is a very great satisfaction to me to be able to bring forward corroborations of her statements.

In the first place, then, a gentleman, a clergyman of

the Church of England, who has been more or less a
medium all his life, has lately developed as a seer, and
has seen some of the spirit emblems, if not with the
same completeness as the lady to whom I allude, at
least with a precision necessary to their identification.
These two persons have seen the same things, both
simultaneously, and when they have been separated by
many miles.   Other persons have beheld spiritual
appearances so analogous to these emblems, that they
entertain no reasonable doubt of the existence of such
things in all the fulness with which they are described,
and I myself rank among the number of these partial
seers.   Secondly, "Confidence," a drawing medium,
one of whose productions is already before the reader,
has been compelled, by the spirit power guiding his
hand, to draw the emblems of certain members of his
family, he never having previously seen any representa-
tion of the sort ; although a seeing medium, who was
in the room at the time, beheld the identical forms he
was in the act of drawing.   The seeress, who beholds
these mystical appearances with the utmost clearness,
describes them as appearing to her in colours of liquid
light, more rich and radiant than earthly jewels.   A

spirit emblem is usually seen behind the person to whom it belongs, the centre of the emblem rising just above the head, and the whole appearance occupying a circumference of several feet. I believe these emblems are ever associated with us—ever borne about with us—as types of our characters and missions, the badges by which we are recognized in the spiritual world, even while we remain on earth.

We have been taught that deep, perhaps inexhaustible arcana dwell in these emblems. Every line, every curve, every shade of colour, every proportion of size, has its mystical meaning, and every new combination has its new and individual characteristics. Let me give a few examples of what I mean.

It will be remembered that the colour Red typifies Love ; Blue, Wisdom ; and Yellow, Light and Life. The union of red and blue forms the different shades of Purple, which is the type of Priesthood, of Power, and of Government.

Spheres signify completion ; and Circles, unity—eternal completion and eternal unity.

The Egg form is indicative of production.

The Moon indicates woman and progress.

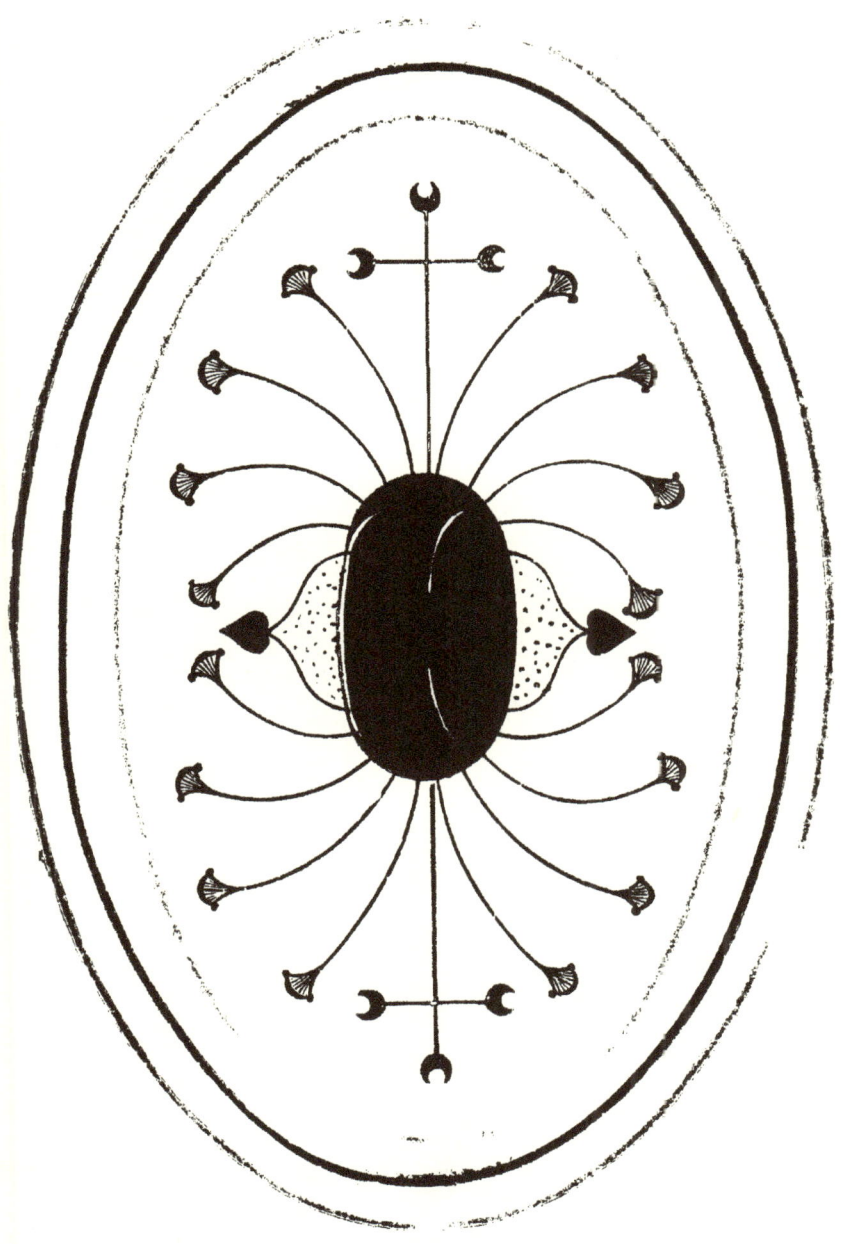

"Sustainer"

Arrows signify influence, generally the influence of speech.

Feathers and dots also indicate influence,—the former influence .over women, or by means of women ; the latter a male influence.

Hearts have a deep meaning, according as they are blazoned. In some emblems, hearts are pierced in the " outer," others in the " inner."

And the Cross, so often found in spirit emblems, is full of significance.

Many of my readers will perhaps see in these spirit emblems a resemblance to heraldic designs, and will smile incredulously at the thought of my being unindebted to heraldry for the ideas I have endeavoured to convey. To such objectors I would remark that the system of heraldry in all probability grew up from a succession of spiritual impressions in the ages when men's minds, not yet materialized by science, presented a broad "upward bearing" to spiritual influences. Truths cannot contradict each other, therefore whatever was true in the past will ultimately be endorsed in the future ; but in all philosophical investigations we need be very cautious not to confound cause and effect. I believe European heraldry to be an earthly reflex of spiritual signs similar in character to those I am attempting to describe ; and that our instinctive yearning after beauty of form and harmony of colour is equally a spiritual prompting and straining after those perfections which the soul alone can perceive. In fact, the ideas of system and government to which spiritual knowledge gives birth, can only with difficulty be described in common language ; although symbolism, when it comes to our aid, often expresses them suggestively and exactly.

I wish now, however, to refer my readers to the first chapter of the Book of the Prophet Ezekiel, which contains the account of a vision that has generally perplexed commentators. All the seers whose attention I have yet drawn to this remarkable chapter, find in it descriptions so analogous to their own experience of emblem-seeing that they feel persuaded the objects shown to the ancient prophet were of a similar character to those which they behold. The whole passage, from the 16th verse to the end of the 21st verse, is indeed very striking in connection with this subject, especially the

PERSONAL SPIRIT-EMBLEM

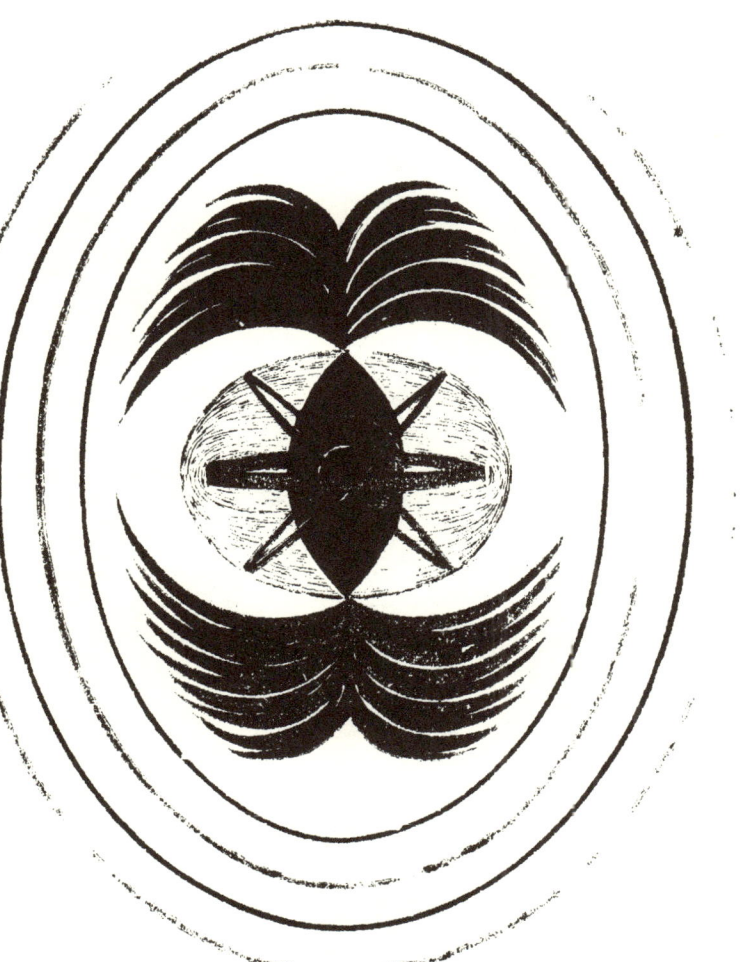

"Innovision"

repetition of the phrase, " For the spirit of the living creature was in the wheels."

Upwards of fifty separate spirit emblems have been seen at different times, a great number of which have been drawn and illuminated from the first rough sketch of the principal seeress, either by herself or under her direction. The exigences of the engraver, however, oblige me to choose for my pages emblems of the simpler sort.

" Sustainer " is the spirit name of a lady who is honoured and beloved by all who know her, and whose human name is a household word in thousands of English homes.

The spirit name " Introvision " was given to a lady some little time before her spirit-seeing faculty became apparent, and also before her emblem, a winged eye, was shown.

" Hopeful " is " Introvision's " son, a child of three years old.

I must also mention that those seers who recognize the emblems, also sometimes see " Crowns of Promise " floating at different distances above the heads of individuals. They describe these crowns as generally appearing to be in harmony with the emblems, that is to say, of the same lustrous spirit substance, and in forms and colours that either correspond or harmonize by contrast with them.   We have been taught that in life our crowns of promise never quite touch our heads, although in moments of soul elevation they approach near, perhaps to within a few inches; while, in an opposite condition, when we are engrossed by the world, or occupied by angry or selfish thoughts, they rise far away, sometimes to the distance of four or five feet.   It has also been remarked that when the individual to whom the crown belongs turns or moves, the crown turns or moves also, even at the greatest distance from the head at which the seers with whom I am acquainted have ever seen them.

It may be well here to observe emphatically that seers draw a broad distinction between a spiritual substance and a material object; and it is a distinction which it is very necessary for the reader to bear in mind.   For my own part, I see in every new revelation which dawns upon us fresh insight into the system of majestic Law and lovely Order which obtains in the spiritual world, and which it is part of the Almighty

"Hopeful"

purpose to reflect on earth. I grant that the reflection is often distorted, as is a pure moonbeam glassed upon a rippling stream ; but instead of cavilling and chafing at the broken image of perfection, we should, I think, do well to admire and study the wondrous plan of progression by antagonism, which Christian Spiritualism daily renders more and more apparent.

Again I must ask the reader not to confuse cause and effect—not to fancy that this crown-seeing is the fond imagining of fantastic minds,—but to retrovert the idea, and inquire whether all Regalia, Orders, and Decorations, may not have proceeded, in the first instance, from spiritual revelations or impressions. Swedenborg, writing on a kindred subject, says :

" The rites and ceremonies observed in the coronation of kings involve such things as are derived from Divine Truth, but the knowledge of these things is at this day lost."

The five illustrations which I must next introduce to the reader are not personal emblems, but symbols of conditions of the human race, past, present, and to come. They were shown in colours of spiritual light, the red and blue brightening from semi-opaque tints to hues of limpid brilliancy, according to the progression of the symbols from No. 1. to No. 5.

It seems to me rather significant and suggestive that the moons, which spirits have told us indicate woman, are not represented as crescent moons, which have yet to grow, but rather as perfect orbs partially eclipsed.

No. 1 typifies Woman hidden in Man; Intellect crowning creation.

No. 2. Woman, the Crown of Creation, displaces Intellect; the Serpent's jealousy is thereby aroused.

No. 3. The Serpent dethrones Woman, and binds her to the Outer.

No. 4. Intellect, no longer a source of discord between Man and Woman, expands and becomes a bond of union. Woman, sustained by Man, is enabled to use her influence (wings) for the elevation of humanity. Both polarized to the Eye of GOD.

No. 5. Man and Woman both polarized to the Eye and Heart of GOD.

SYMBOLS.—No. 1.

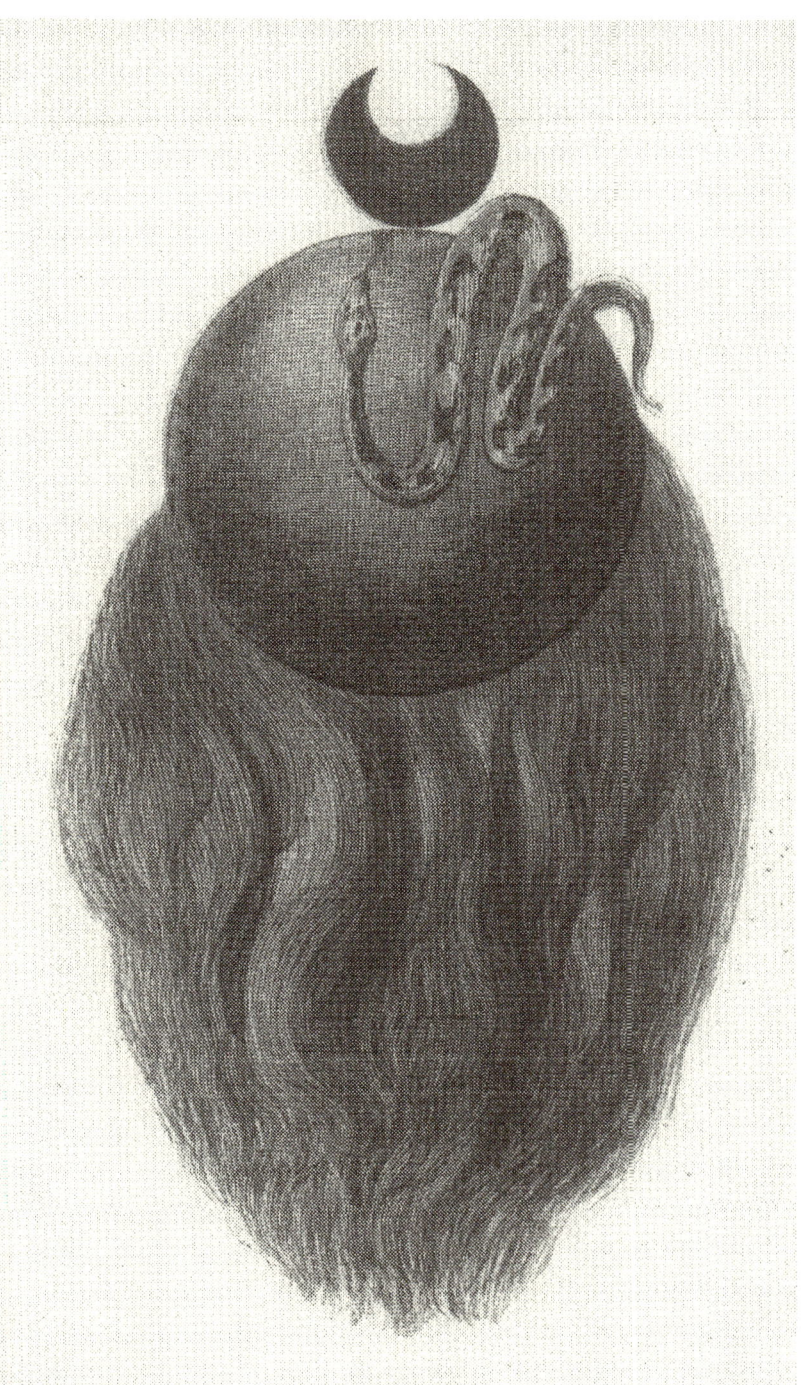

SYMBOLS.—No. 2.

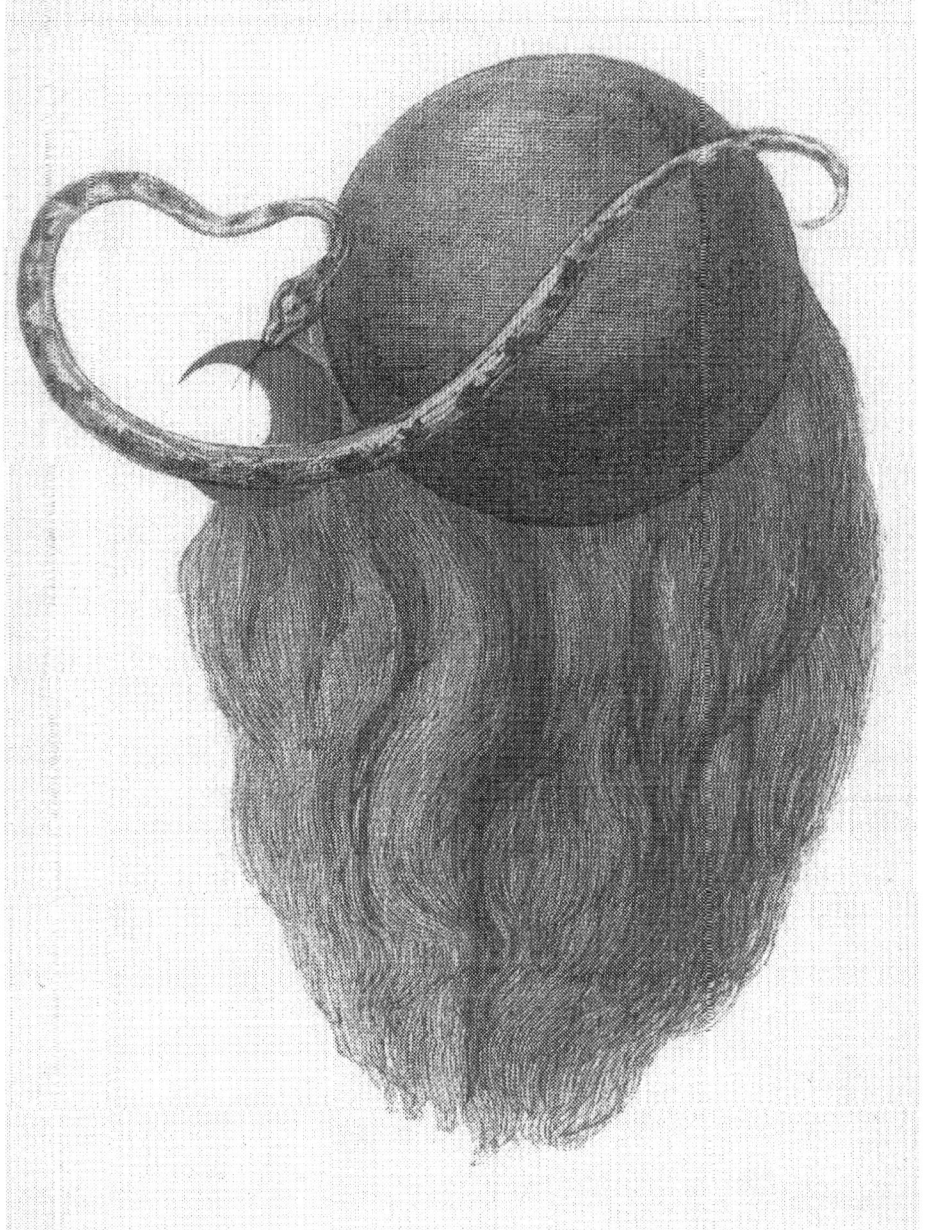

SYMBOLS.—No. 3.

SYMBOLS.—No. 4.

SYMBOLS.—No. 5.

CHAPTER VIII.

PERSONAL ATMOSPHERES.—PRAYER.—THE BIRTH OF HARMONY.

IN his last chapter a writer generally gathers up the threads of his discourse, and endeavours, whether successfully or not, to round off his work with something like finish, and to leave it in a state that is called complete. But one who attempts to write on Spiritual Phenomena can never, properly speaking, "finish" his task, or indulge in the flattering idea that the work is "complete." Even while these pages have been passing through the press, fresh information and new revelations have crowded upon me, all tending to illustrate and develope the theories I have already mentioned.

I find, from the Seeress to whom the psychical atmospheres are so frequently visible—and I may observe that these atmospheres have been seen by several other mediums of my acquaintance—that not only are they to be distinguished by infinite gradations of colour and density, or of ethereal lightness, but that in some instances these personal atmospheres are thrown off in waves, in others by jets. It would appear that the delicate organization of insects renders them keenly susceptible of these different influences, and that persons whose atmospheres jet, are more likely to suffer from stinging insects than are any others. We have also been told that, to be a tender nurse or skilful physician, a person needs to have what the spirits call a healing atmosphere; and a yellow scarlet that comes forth in waves is indicative of this quality. Such an atmosphere, typifying a union of love and life, is represented as possessing and imparting certain magnetic properties conducive to health, and as being peculiarly open to the reception of mental impressions from Healing Spirits.

Just as healing properties are, in some instances, conveyed through the means of these atmospheres, so are diseases not unfrequently imparted by atmospheres antagonistic to health. The Seeress to whom I have more particularly alluded in connection with this subject, tells me that from past experience she can distinguish between the appearances of certain contagious diseases, as they show themselves in spots on the subtle atmosphere emanating from persons about to be attacked with those specific maladies.

Moreover, she informs me that our own personal atmospheres are all more or less affected by the atmospheres of those friends or relations who appear to exercise influence over us. For instance, certain persons have on or about their atmospheres patches or coatings (visible to her) of other atmospheres, which she has in many instances identified as belonging to members of their family, or friends with whom they were intimately associated.

In fact, the psychical atmosphere may be considered a connecting something between spirit and matter, and renders the privileged Seer a subtle detector of character, health, and influences.

I mention these circumstances for my readers to theorize from if they please. And I have to add that the Seeress whom I have so often mentioned beholds atmospheres about trees, flowers, and various other objects, and especially about all precious stones. She once assured me that she saw entangled in the atmosphere of a certain diamond ring, the atmospheres of its present and three previous wearers. Perhaps the

Bible history of the Urim and Thummim may become, by a recognition of crystal-seeing and subtle atmospheres, understandable through our human reason; and even the strange stories of talismans which have floated down the stream of time, and been looked on as idle traditions, may prove at last to have had more truth than fable in them.

Later experiences have deepened my conviction of the wide distinction which must always be made between incorruptible spiritual substances, which are not to be recognized by our physical organs, and the most subtle and delicate of material forms. Mediums perpetually receive communications from spirits in various modes, which, if described, would never change the opinions of a sceptic, because in these cases the inter-course is purely that of spirit with spirit; but when me-diumship is of such a character that—as in the instance of Mr. Home—it permits spirit to incarnate itself, then manifestations result which can be recognized by any spectator. Possibly these incarnations take place from an appropriation of elements which exist in the atmo-sphere, they being acted upon through the Medium by vital, magnetic, and electric forces. Something of the same sort also occurs when the raps are made, and when heavy articles are lifted and suspended in the air by invisible means, as I have repeatedly seen done, because in these instances the manifestations are apparent to our outward senses, and for this to be the case a union of spirit and matter must take place. Allusion has already been made to the circumstance that feet, which tread upon the earth, and hands, which work for the body, represent the outer of humanity; and I think it is a significant fact that in recent manifestations the hand appears to have been the member most readily incarnated.

In the foregoing various descriptions of spiritual phenomena the senses of sight, hearing, and touch have been those through which the manifestations have become most absolutely apparent; but I have now to add that the sense of smell has to be associated with the other faculties, as witness for the occurrence of super-ordinary circumstances.

One of the most highly developed mediums with whom I am privileged to be acquainted, frequently emits from her person, and especially from the ends of her fingers, the most delicious scent of roses. The phenomenon generally occurs suddenly, and at periods of great exhaustion of the psychical fluid, consequent on powerful spiritual manifestations having taken place; and occasionally it is followed by the odour of sweet briar. To the facts I am now narrating at least a score of credible witnesses are ready to bear testimony; and their evidence would, of course, remind the reader of some traditions associated with the names of certain saints, of the truth of which we are too apt—it may be—altogether to doubt. Nor is the medium to whom I more particularly allude the only one I have to mention as being thus singularly gifted. A child medium, a little girl whose mediumship is now developing, emits the rose odour; and we have been informed that this emission of flower scents is about to be strikingly developed as a token and result of certain capacities of mediumship.

Indeed, our spirit friends have instructed us that every human being so far represents a trinity of flowers as to have three flowers belonging to him, the scents of which are capable, under certain circumstances, of becoming apparent to the physical sense. The three odours correspond to the outer, the inner, and the innermost of our being; the outer manifesting itself by far the more readily. It is a singular circumstance that the medium in whom the rose and sweet briar odours are so palpable, has herself been able in numerous instances to distinguish the spirit-flower odours of other mediums, though imperceptible to their friends in general,—such, for instance, as the scent of magnolia, violet, mignonette, and scabious; the fact of her really having done so not resting merely on her assertion, but having been in several instances confirmed by spirit messages. Perhaps it is not quite out of place to remark that the rose appears to be peculiarly associated with symbolic spirit teaching,—as if its heart-shaped petals, its love colour, and its spherical form, were replete with subtle meanings.

My task is drawing towards its close, and yet I have still many things which I earnestly desire to say. The object of this book will have been quite mistaken if it tends to induce any one to seek for spiritual manifestations out of vain curiosity, or with a mind unspiritualized by religious feelings. People who are not called to take part in the work so strangely opening before mediums, would be wise to receive evidence with as little personal experience as possible; but if, from a certain stubbornness of character, they must see, and hear, and examine for themselves, I entreat them to do so prayerfully and carefully. I entreat them never, under any circumstances, to hold parley with evil or " undeveloped " spirits, and always to use an exorcism, worded and heart-dictated in the name of the Triune God, whenever they are receiving spirit messages or beholding spiritual manifestations. Let them not smile the incredulous smile of infidelity at my words; I have *known* evil spirits to be exorcized and silenced when they have been tried* in faith and found wanting. And I have known prayer for spiritual assistance and divine protection to be answered on the instant in a most astonishing manner. I believe that the reason why the visits of sceptics to professional mediums have so often proved unsatisfactory is, that a party of strangers, among whom may be many discordant elements of nature, rarely forms a quite harmonious circle; and even a perfectly harmonious circle is not likely to obtain striking manifestations until repeated sittings have polarized the individuals to each other, and the

1st Epistle General of St. John, iv.

attendant spirits have become used to amalgamate the different atmospheres.

More than once in these pages have I alluded to the revelations which have been made to us on the subject of prayer ; and I have an incident to narrate in illustration of the theme, which with some minds may have more weight than chapters of theorizing. And yet, after all, it is only one among scores of kindred instances. A lady, a medium who, under mesmerism, quickly passes into the highest stages of clairvoyance, was clairvoyante in my presence. After we had listened to some very elevated and astonishing revelations from her lips, she paused for a time, while we, the lookers-on, remained also silent. Presently she exclaimed with a sort of rapture, "Oh ! there are such numbers of spirits—there are forty come into the room together, and they have brought A—— a prayer ! " Now I should mention that previously to this circumstance occurring, three or four different prayers had been dictated by spirits for the use of individuals, and therefore, knowing at once what was meant, I procured pen and ink on the instant, and took down, from the rapid dictation of the medium, those words which were shown to her in letters of light

by one of A——'s guardian angels. They formed a
prayer so beautiful that it is worthy to be placed side by
side with some of the finest Collects of the Prayer-Book ;
but at the same time this prayer is so personal, so
much a supplication for peculiar help under peculiar
circumstances, that, although it has been placed at my
disposal, I decline to lay it bare to the chances of
ridicule. But the striking illustration of the efficacy
of prayer which this incident afforded remains to be
told. During the pause in the *clairvoyante's* discourse
A—— had silently prayed that a form of supplication
suitable to his individual need might be given him,
though probably not daring to imagine how promptly
the boon would be granted.

The heart must indeed be far from God which an
event like this does not solemnize.

I have already said that, properly speaking, there
can be no conclusion, no real ending to this little book.
I believe that changes are coming upon the earth,
through spiritual instrumentalities, of which materialists
have no idea. To many ardent souls the grey dawn of
the better day is already apparent, although they cannot
conjecture what the brilliancy of its noon may be ; but

Christian Spiritualists are permitted to see something more. To them that grey dawn shines upon the foundation-stones of a New Jerusalem which is indeed coming down from Heaven, in a fashion far different from the guise long imaged by interpreters of prophecy, and yet faithfully like the promised glory. Nay, Christian Spiritualists sometimes feel that they are already dwellers in that city which "had no need of the sun, neither of the moon to shine in it; for the glory of God did lighten it, and the Lamb is the light thereof."

To some among us a degree of the reality of heavenly things has already come; and to all mankind I believe there is approaching the Advent of that State which is symbolized in Comfort's spirit drawing, entitled "The Birth of Harmony."

ADDENDA.

ADDENDA.

UNDER this head I class various communications which kind friends have transmitted to me while the foregoing pages were passing through the press, and some other apposite illustrations of Spiritualism. The first letter I shall extract is from an Officer in the Army.

DEAR MRS. CROSLAND,

Having been converted at your house from the veriest sceptic in spiritual communications to a believer in them, by means of phenomena which I there witnessed for the first time,—though since then I have witnessed similar manifestations at the houses of several of my own friends,—I think you will be interested in the following experience, which brings the truth of spirit communication to a very simple question : either it is true, or I, my friend Mr. ——, and three of my family are wilful deceivers.

You may perhaps consider this prelude unnecessary ; but, I can assure you, from my own inquiry I find so many who reject all evidence in favour of spiritualism, and bring such absurd arguments against it, and, in spite of proof, still so wilfully adhere to their opinions, which are in most cases formed from knowing but little of the subject, that I think a slight preface may not be out of place for the benefit of those obstinate non-reasoners, who by their partiality remind me of an Irish judge, who would never hear evidence on more than one side, lest he should be puzzled in his decision.

I was in town a few evenings ago at Mr. ——'s ; after we had been consulting on matters unconnected with spiritualism, he asked me if I would sit at a little table, and see if any communication would be given. We did sit, and the table very soon began tilting with great power. After it had done so six or seven times I used a little pressure to try and stop it, but found the resistance in the table so great, that I at once knew something was to be indicated by this unusual demonstration.

The movements continued until Mr.—— said "Seventy-three tilts" (for he, not I, had counted), and I at once conjectured that 73 was indicated as my mother's age, and a signal from her, she having died about three or four weeks previously. When I said " that was the age of my mother," the affirmative was given by means of the table. I then asked if any message was intended, when the following was the response : " You will wish for some proof of my being a spirit and happy, for father does not believe ;—that you know."

I then said, " Will you give me some proof that will convince father ?"

Answer : " Yes, tell him to look in my top workbox ;

'he will find a lock of hair given to me by him before we were married."

Question: "When and where was the lock of hair given?"

A.: "At my father's, about ten months before my marriage."

Q.: "Will you give me some other proof that will convince my father?"

A.: "When he gave me the lock of hair he said——"

The words my father used were then given. I wrote down each question and answer of this communication. You are aware Mr. —— did not know a single member of my family, and I had not been to my father's home for more than a day for several years. I had never to my knowledge seen the inside of a workbox of my mother's, nor did I know where this particular one was, nor in whose possession. Two days afterwards I went home, told my family the occasion of my visit, and then went with three of them as witnesses into my late mother's room. We there found the workbox, which was locked, and had been kept by my mother in a drawer quite private for many years. Upon opening the box we found some papers, and under them a piece of old paper, folded up, in which was a lock of hair—my father's name being written on the paper. My father remembered the circumstance of giving the hair, but, fifty-four years having passed, he could not say what his words had been.

All my family were sceptics before this occurrence, but

now, of course, they cannot disbelieve with such proo~
before them. My father, who had been fretting day anc
night for my mother, seemed after this event to look upon
death with a different feeling; he is now much more
resigned and composed.

I must apologize for the length of this letter, but trust
that the cause will plead my excuse, and remain,

Dear Mrs. Crosland,

Your deeply indebted and sincere friend,

1st May, 1857.   " CANDOUR."

A letter from a lady narrates spiritual experiences of
a different order :—

May 5th, 1857.

MY DEAR MRS. CROSLAND,

I believe our former acquaintance would have
justified my writing to you, if I had not heard from dear
Miss——, that any fresh thought or experience might be
welcome on that beautiful subject which fills so much of
all our thoughts, and which must occupy them until its
effects are universally seen in the advent of Christ's
kingdom on earth.

I am not a medium myself, but six persons in the
house are more or less developed, and through them, and
by various means, some interesting knowledge has been
conveyed to me, some part of which, relating to the process of spiritual communication through mediums, I should
like to send you.

It appears that in almost all cases of grown persons becoming mediums, a process compared by the spirits to the *Exodus* is gone through. It is likely that, in the restoration of the whole world to the will of God, which will be the second advent of the Lord, the human race collectively must pass through this process. I learned a good deal from Misses —— and —— on this subject, and very likely they have given you what little we have learned here; but it is interesting to compare different experiences. One of my servants is now in a state of change from one phase of mediumship to another. Just as she was passing from her first state (and at that time she had not heard a word of the Egyptian journey) she dreamed that she gathered up on the sea-shore, stones on which were carved various animals. Two of these stones, the representations of a lion and a camel, she gave to me, but kept none herself. I took these two, saying that they were Egyptian, and I would take them home. The next day this dream was explained through the other mediums to imply that she would lose her mediumship for the present, and that it would pass to myself.

Soon after this I became ill, and, during my illness, was told that it would contribute to my becoming a medium; that I was then passing through the Red Sea, and should soon reach the other side. In due time I was "in the wilderness," then at the bitter waters, and so on. During this time many strange and contradictory statements seemed to be made, and at length it was whispered to one of the mediums in the house, that "when any one was in the wilderness, good spirits found it difficult to get near ; only those closely related, and *alike*, could approach near enough to see the state of, or communicate with, the travellers."   This seemed to imply that a change in the magnetic state was symbolized by the passage of the Red Sea and wilderness, and I begged one of my spirit friends to draw for me figures representing the directions of the magnetic lines (or vibrations) in persons who were mediums and in those who were not.

I traced out two figures, and my little girl (aged 10) was made to add the third and fourth, and to draw the lines.

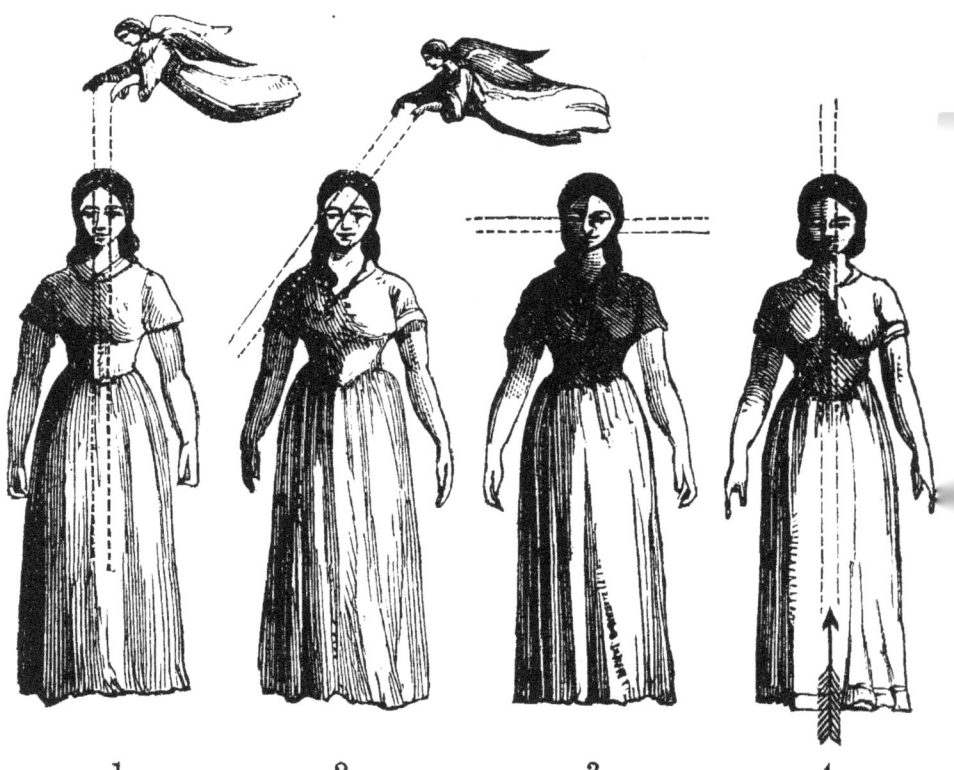

1   2   3   4

1. A perfect medium for good spirits.

2. Partially a medium ; in this state all kinds of false impressions are conveyed to the mind.

3. Not a medium at all ; the magnetism is parallel with the earth's horizon.

4. A medium under the influence of evil spirits ; the magnetism is directed in an opposite current to that which conveys the Holy influence.

It appears by these little sketches, and by other explanations given, that one in a transition state, or passing from 2 to 1, is *in the wilderness*, when spiritual truth, or food, can come but scantily and imperfectly, mixed with falsehood and bitterness ;—that the attainment of the state drawn in No. 1 is the reaching the promised land, when the medium transmits the vital love of God as it comes direct from the highest source, and is thus *linked on* to the infinite series of angels and spirits, through whom the glory is poured even from the Lamb in the centre of the throne.

It was also told us that the transverse, or *diamagnetic* state of the spiritual world (including spirits on our earth) constituted the cross of Christ. When we are all fitting temples of the Holy Spirit, and receive it without refraction or falsification, this horizontal magnetism will cease, and the Lord will be taken down from the cross.

Another little diagram was made representing the various ways in which the religion of Christ has been modified by the direction in which it has been received ;

of course the perpendicular line is the only *true* one,

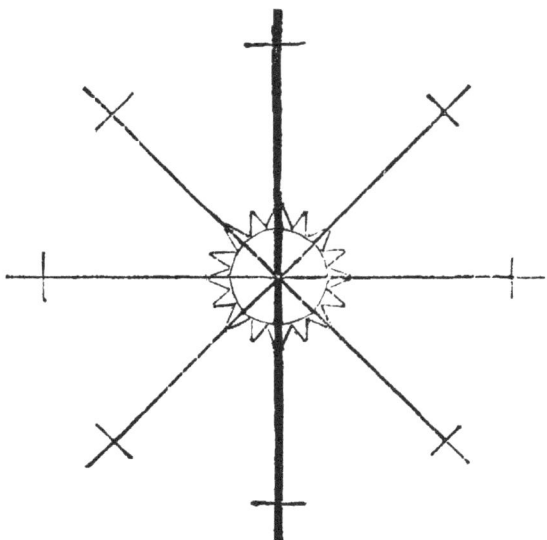

but there are various approaches and varieties. The central sun, I think, represented the Lord, the union of the divine and human, but this could not be given clearly through my little girl; dear Miss —— will readily detect any fallacy, and supply any deficiency.

If these things are true, we see why the highest organs, those which place us in connection with the better world and with Our Father, are on the top of the head.

Whether the promise of mediumship given to me will be fulfilled I do not of course know. We are told that other conditions besides the direction of the magnetism must be fulfilled. It was written through my tiny girl, seven years old,—

" Light comes from God, and passes through spirits and mediums. When there are no mediums the world is in darkness."

This must be " the light shown in darkness, and the darkness *comprehended* it not." I know there have been discussions as to the meaning of the word " comprehend." It seems to imply reception and transmission.

Believe me, dear Mrs. Crosland, with very kindest remembrances to ——, yours very sincerely,

"DEPENDENCE."

The third letter I shall here insert is from a clergyman, to whom allusion has been made in this volume.

DEAR MRS. CROSLAND,

The sledge-hammer which was aimed at our devoted heads, will, I think, be a weapon in our own hands. Inclosed you will find a literal translation of the entire paragraph in which those texts occur, and a few annotations. It must be remembered that the ancient division of both Testaments was into paragraphs, each generally comprising one subject. Consequently the entire paragraph is required, in order to understand the writer's meaning. The quotation from St. John seems to me the *coup de grace*, and, curiously enough, exactly corroborates Swedenborg's statement respecting the "last times," although he seldom quotes the epistles. I should not wonder if we were, after demolishing our adversary's position, to build the materials into a strong fortification for ourselves. I have already found five or six passages that are much more in our favour than those already quoted seem to be against us. (The raps have been going on all the time while I was writing the translation.)

—— will assuredly be charged with texts, and ought to be met with her own weapons. I have just noted one or two, all from the Epistles of St. Paul :—

Rom. viii. 5, 34. 1 Cor. xii. 4 to 12. 1 Cor. xiv. 32, 39. (This will be wanted against one of the opposition.) Heb. i. 14. Heb. xii. 22, 23, 24.

I think that it would be useful if you could look up every passage that relates, or seems to relate, to such matters, and we will get at the truth of them before Friday. I am already doing so, but shall certainly miss some. Did not —— make use of some passages? I should like Mr. —— to see my translations, in order to have his testimony to their accuracy, or —— will refuse to receive them.—Yours very sincerely, S.

ACTS XVI. 16.

" It happened, that as we were going unto prayer [or, *into an oratory*], a certain young-girl having a spirit of Python* met us, who afforded much gain to her masters,

---

* Python (Πυθών) was the name of the serpent killed by Apollo at the spot called from it Pytho. The Pythian oracles were given from thence. In the time of Plutarch, A.D. 140, ventriloquists were called Pythones, and Pythonissæ. This was some oracular spirit connected with the heathen deity Apollo. The spirit of prophecy (προφητεία) is frequently mentioned as a direct gift from the Holy Spirit. See—

1 Cor. xii. 10.—" To another prophecy, in the same Spirit.

1 Cor. xiv. 5.—"Greater is he that prophesieth than he that speaketh with tongues."

Eph. iii. 5.—" As it is now revealed unto the holy Apostles and Prophets by the Spirit."

Eph. iv. 11.—" And He gave some apostles, and some prophets, and some evangelists."

For Prophetess, Luke ii. 36.—"And there was Anna, a prophetess," &c.

Acts xxi. 8, 9.—" And having entered into the house of Philip

soothsaying. She, having followed-closely Paul and us, cried-aloud, saying, 'These men are servants of the God, the Highest, who announce to us a path of salvation.' And this she did for many days. But Paul, being vexed, and having turned about, spake to the spirit, 'I command thee, in the name of Jesus Christ, to come out from her.' And it came out that same hour."

1 Tim. iii. 16.

¶ VII. "And confessedly, great is the mystery of piety ; God was manifested in flesh, made-righteous in spirit, seen by angels, proclaimed in nations, believed on in the world, taken up in glory. But the Spirit definitely [or, by appointment] saith, that in later times* some will apostatize from the faith, attending to deceitful [or, wandering, erring] spirits, and to the doctrines of demons speaking lies in hypocrisy, cauterized in their own con-

the Evangelist, being of the seven, we abode by him. And to him were four virgin daughters that prophesied."
1 Thess. v. 20.—"Set not at naught prophecy."

* Matt. xxiv. 23-4.—"Then, if any one say to you, Behold, here the Christ, or there, believe not. For there shall arise false Christs and false Prophets, and they shall give great signs and miracles, so as to mislead if it (were) possible even the chosen. . . . .
—— v. 34. Amen I say to you, *this generation shall not pass-away, until all these* (things) *happen.* The heaven and the earth shall pass-away, but My words shall not pass-away." A.D. 33.
1 John, ii. 18.—"Little children, *it is the* LAST *hour ;* and as ye heard that the Antichrist cometh, and *now* many Antichrists have arisen ; from thence we know that it is the last hour. They went out from us, but were not of us," &c. A.D. 90.

science, forbidding to marry, (commanding) to* abstain
from meats, which (things) the God established unto
receiving with thanksgiving by the faithful, and those
who have comprehended the truth. For every institution
of God (is) good, and nothing (is) to be cast away (that is)
received with thanksgiving, for it is made-holy through
the word of God and of (His) communion. Suggesting
these (things) to the brethren, thou shalt be a good
minister of Jesus Christ, nourished in the words of the
faith, and of the good doctrine which thou hast closely
followed. Now these profane and anile counsels re-
nounce ; but exercise thyself unto piety." A.D. 66.

The following narrative is from the pen of a gentleman
who has been in the habit of receiving spiritual communications for many years, and who is the son of a very
distinguished deceased statesman :—

"In the year 1841, on Wednesday, the 27th of January,
I attended, by invitation, at a ball which was given by
the late king of the French, Louis Philippe, at the Tui-
leries. During the course of the evening I returned from
one of the saloons to the reception-room, where the king
and queen were seated on two chairs, with the princesses,
ambassadors' wives, and *dames de la cour*, on forms to the
right of and behind them ; whilst a part of the room was
fenced off with red ropes passing through the heads of
iron rods let into the floor, to make room for two sets of
quadrilles that were being danced before their majesties.

* Rom. xiv. 6-14 ; 1 Cor. viii. 8, &c. &c. &c. ; Col. ii. 8-23.

" I came to that end of the space roped off for the dancers, which was nearest the windows and on the right side of the king and royal family, and whilst there I turned round to admire the head-dresses and appearances of the ladies of the court, when I was particularly struck by the contrast between the Duchesse de Nemours, who was very beautiful, and who wore nothing upon her head but a wreath of roses, and the Duchesse d'Orléans, who, though short and plain, was full of dignity, and wore in her hair a very splendid ornament of diamonds. I am not aware that anything else was passing in my mind at the time, except that I was very much annoyed by the crowding and pressing of the company around me, and felt a sensation of disgust at Louis Philippe himself, and at *liberal* monarchies in general, for allowing such squeezing and such vulgarity in their presence for the sake of popularity.

All of a sudden I heard in my right ear a beautiful voice, like that of an angel, much slighter even than that of a child, which commenced singing to me the following lines :—

> Brille, cour,—brille !
> Qui pauvres gens pille !
> Mais de près et de soudain
> Vient une forte main,
> Qui couronne arrache,
> Et fausse modestie tâche,
> Et diamants et or grappille.

" I give you the lines as they succeeded each other, but I must mention that, as is usually the case when any of this kind of phenomena occur to me, on account of the affecting beauty of the tones and the preternatural nature of the communication, I became extremely anxious and nervous about hearing and recollecting accurately that which was being spoken to me, and judging whether it was the voice of truth or a mere illusion; and when I heard the words 'de près,' being then of opinion that the throne of Louis Philippe had triumphed over all republicanism, and that nothing could injure him, at least in Paris, where he was supported by the army and by the National Guard as well, I became doubtful and agitated, when, as often has occurred to me in similar circumstances, I perceived, but as from another voice or in another manner, the words *de loin* substituted for *de près*, which agreed better with my notions, at that time, that if any danger threatened Louis Philippe, it would come from the Legitimists and probably from the neighbourhood of Bordeaux, or at least from La Vendée. Whilst, however, perplexed at this double message, I saw in a vision, issuing from the crowd of courtiers immediately opposite to the king, the hand and half-naked arm of a man, *en chemise*, like *une main d'ouvrier*, the fist of which was clenched, and it appeared to approach and menace the king. When the voice ceased, I was left in a state of great awe and wonder. But I returned home unable to divine what duty this singular vision imposed upon me. I was in great anxiety of mind for some time, but at last I determined to do nothing more than write it to one of my sisters;

ﬁearing that, after all, the Almighty might be tempting me with a delusion; and that I might only expose myself to pity and ridicule, and perhaps make a goose of myself if I sought to make it known to any great people.

"It was not till the crash of empires and kingdoms came in 1848, and with it the downfall of Louis Philippe's dynasty, that I understood this vision and prophecy, and saw their truth; and I then thought how blind I was and hard of belief, like the Apostles when hearing their Lord's parables of old, not to have understood them immediately. There is one line, however, in the prophecy —'et fausse modestie tâche'—which I acknowledge I do not yet accurately know how to apply, or with certainty.

"Happening to be at Odell Castle in the year 1845 or 1846, attending on the death-bed of one of my aunts, there being no accommodation for me in the castle, I slept at the vicarage belonging to the Rev. Mr. Alston. His lady belongs, or belonged, to Mr. Irving's church in London, and having mentioned to her the above circumstance, she asked me to write the verses in her Album, which I did. My sister remembers my having written them to her in 1841, but, being little curious in such things, she believes that she destroyed the letter."

The following paragraphs were sent me by a literary friend, who considered the anecdote first mentioned a curious illustration of partial spirit incarnation :—

"Aubrey tells in his Miscellanies of a Sir Walter

Q

Long, of Draycot, who, having a son by a first wife, and
being married to a second, a woman of much artifice and
ambition, was induced by her to disinherit his eldest son
for the sake of his younger children. 'She laid the scene
for doing this at Bath, at the Assizes, where was her
brother, Sir Egremond Thynne, an eminent serjeant-at-
law, who drew up the writing; and his clerk was to sit
up all night to engross it. As he was writing he perceived a shadow on the parchment from the candle; he
looked up, and there appeared a hand, which immediately
vanished. He was startled at it, but thought it might
be only his fancy, being sleepy; so he writ on. By-and-
by a fine white hand interposed between the writing
and the candle (he could discover it was a woman's hand),
but vanished as before. With that the clerk threw
down his pen and would engross no more, but goes and
tells his master of it, and absolutely refused to do it.'
Aubrey goes on to relate that the iniquitous arrangement
was made; but after Sir Walter's death, the trustees of
his first wife compelled the heir to surrender a part of
the estates to the disinherited brother. 'This,' he says,
'was about the middle of the reign of King James the
First.' "

"There was once a remarkable case in Scotland. It
occurred in 1720, the subject being a boy, a younger son
of the Lord Torphichen of that day. It is related that
the family had to watch him, and take hold of him by
his skirts as he floated off into the air. He always knew
beforehand when it would take place."

The following is portion of a letter which appeared in the "Times" of May 2nd, 1857.

WITCHCRAFT.

To the Editor of the Times.

Sir,—Will you permit me to offer a few remarks in your columns on a subject just now exciting some little curiosity—that of witchcraft ?

In his interesting communications to your paper "E. E." has indeed directed attention to "a dark corner" of the human mind. Of late years, however, strange as it may appear, conviction has been growing in the minds of not a few attentive and candid observers, that the darkness which your correspondent so deplores lies less in the belief in witchcraft than in the disbelief of the real facts on which it is founded. That much gross error is mixed up with the popular belief in what is termed witchcraft is undoubtedly true, but equally true may it be that rejection of the subject as mere superstition of the vulgar is proof, not of enlightenment, but of insufficient knowledge—of ignorance of the deeper arcana of nature's book.

Those who have studied the modern phenomena of mesmerism, clairvoyance, and others more startling still, and who have paid attention to the instances of spontaneous development of these phenomena, abounding throughout the literature, the chronicles, and legends of antique and mediæval times, are struck with a sameness so complete between the old phenomena and the new as to be irresistibly led to infer the existence of an occult law to which they must be reducible.

To account for this sameness on the ground of "the obstinate vitality of tradition" will not do, for it is a sameness far less of the letter than of the spirit, an essential identity discernible through much superficial dissimilarity, and existing not only between the old supernatural (so called) manifestations and those of the present day, but also between those of the most widely different and distant regions—between the witchcraft of rural localities in England and the sorceries of the African deserts and of the forests and prairies of the New World. May not this propensity, seen so powerfully to exist in the human mind towards the mysterious, point to correlative facts dimly glimmering through the vast, the unexplored tract of nature's realm? That it is not to be corrected by education, that it may be found in the highest and best-balanced minds, might be proved by abundant examples.   .   .   .   .   .

I am, Sir, yours obediently,   V.

PRINTED BY COX AND WYMAN, GREAT QUEEN STREET.

CPSIA information can be obtained
at www.ICGtesting.com
Printed in the USA
BVHW052213120922
646875BV00003B/36